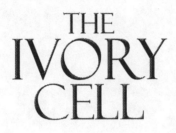

THE
IVORY
CELL

THE
IVORY
CELL

❧NEVINE MILLER❧

authorHOUSE®

AuthorHouse™
1663 Liberty Drive
Bloomington, IN 47403
www.authorhouse.com
Phone: 1-800-839-8640

Published by AuthorHouse   05/31/2013

ISBN: 978-1-4817-5874-1 (sc)
ISBN: 978-1-4817-5873-4 (hc)
ISBN: 978-1-4817-5872-7 (e)

Library of Congress Control Number: 2013909816

I dedicate this book to my three children:
Nimet, Nihal, and Hassan Mazloum. With all my love.

CHAPTER 1

I was the third daughter to be born to Nahed Said and Hussein Sirry in Cairo, the last child after my sisters Ihsan and Adila, on June 8th, 1929. In that particular era, yet another baby girl might have been a source of regret for my large and close extended family. But if my parents had longed for a boy to carry on the family name, I was none the wiser. I felt myself to be adored by all, and my childhood was enormously happy, part of a loving, busy household filled with company and color. As playmates I had my two sisters, nicknamed Nini and Doddy, and we were entertained and doted upon by a benign army of servants and nannies. Frankly, I see now that I was a bit of a spoiled brat.

We lived in one of the nicer parts of Cairo, in the neighborhood of Zamalek, a lovely spot that had been built for British dignitaries. Egypt at the time was under British protectorate, and the Zamalek houses had been built for British dignitaries. Ours was a two-story home, white with green shutters and a lovely garden. Charming and cozy, it had a fireplace in every room—a practical British tradition because there was no other means of heat during the chilly winter evenings. The first floor was a reception area with a shiny grand piano, a big dining room, and my father's study. But we mostly lived upstairs, where we studied and played in the bedrooms and the sunny family room.

My mother and father, like the well born children of their day, were united by their parents in an arranged marriage. The young couple did not meet until the day of their wedding, and there was much anxiety for both. Because my father had been told that his wife-to-be closely resembled her father the prime minister, he was much relieved to see that his very pretty bride did not sport a mustache. She in turn was charmed by him. He was a fine looking and bright young man from a good family in Egypt. He appeared to be stern and reserved but underneath he had a great sense of humor and a big heart which he tried to hide behind his abrupt manner and straight to the point speech.

My mother and father spent their wedding night in the family's unoccupied house, and as was customary, my grandparents telephoned in the morning to see how the night had passed. The maid answered and responded brightly that all was well: the two lovebirds were upstairs singing!

Although such a concept seems counter-intuitive in today's world, arranged marriages were more often than not brilliantly happy, as this one was. My sisters' arranged marriages, at 16 and 18, were also long-lived and successful. My own first marriage, a love match at 18, did not fare so well.

 C3

My mother's family dated back to Muhammad Ali, the Albanian warlord who is regarded as the founder of modern Egypt. Muhammad Ali was commander of the Ottoman army that was sent to drive Napoleon's forces out of Egypt. But with the French withdrawal, the canny warlord seized power himself and forced the Ottoman Sultan to recognize him as Governor of Egypt. Muhammad Ali's reign beginning in 1805 encompassed a period of reform and modernization that led to Egypt's becoming one of the most civilized countries outside of Europe.

Muhammad Ali brought to Egypt his Turkish harem, "splendid and well-kept" young women, according to the literature of the day. In order to secure his power among the most affluent Egyptians, the new governor bestowed upon each of them a woman from his own harem to have in marriage, along with a dowry of 1,000 acres, or 1000 "feddans". Thus, the origin of my mother's family fortune could be traced back to one of the first Turkish women married in Egypt.

My maternal grandmother was a marvelous woman, very refined, who spoke all the European languages. Her husband, my grandfather, Muhammad Said Pasha, served as prime minister. But he was also a gambler and evidently not a successful one. He lost a lot of money, and then died suddenly leaving my grandmother burdened with his vast debt. Traditionally in that place and time, a man's debts would die with him. However, my grandmother, who as a descendant of a woman from Muhammad Ali's harem had plenty of her own money, decided to honor his debts. The family congregated to help her with finances, but there was still much left to pay off. For the rest of her life she continued to winnow down the debt, finally becoming free of it only two years before her death in 1960. She was a fantastic lady, really, with a crystal-clear moral compass.

Her daughter, my dear mother, was schooled in the home by tutors, spoke several languages, and had a beautiful soprano voice. She grew to be a lovely woman, with an independent and questing mind that would become one of her most marked traits. One of my earliest memories is of my mother kneeling by my bed to kiss me good night as she made her way to an evening at the palace. She wore a "yashmak", a white veil that covered her hair and face, and only her beautiful black eyes shone through. As was customary, my mother wore the yashmak whenever she left the house. Later, she was one of the first women in Egypt to give up the veil. She simply decided she no longer wanted to wear it, a very advanced notion in such an aristocratic family. The veil was a Koranic symbol, a sign of distinction and protection for upper-class women; my grandmother wore a white veil whenever she left the house until the day she died.

When my mother told my father of her wish to stop wearing the veil, he rather surprised her, and said, "Fine. Take it off." She was thus liberated, although she continued to wear her yashmak whenever she had dinner at the palace with her niece and my first cousin Safinaz Zulficar, better known as Farida, Queen of Egypt, and wife of King Farouk.

Yes, my mother's family was quite storied. My mother's brother, my wonderful uncle Mahmoud Said, was a renowned artist who played a central role in the development of modern art in Egypt. Mahmoud has been dead some fifty years, but recently one of his paintings sold for more than $2 million at a Dubai auction. Painting for my uncle was a sideline, however; his real work was as a lawyer and judge. He never made much money, and I always wondered why he never sold any of his beautiful artwork. He told me that as a man of the law he could not imagine being an impartial judge to a buyer of his art. Like all of my family he was an honorable man, one of the finest I've ever known.

My father's family on the other hand, was of Egyptian origin, extraordinarily wealthy and accomplished though they were. My paternal grandfather, Ismail Sirry Pasha, had worked as an engineer in France, and was responsible for much of the construction in the Carmargue in the south of France, and was given a beautiful house there by the French government in recognition of his talents. He later became Minister of Public Works in Egypt. My father, like his father, was educated at the prestigious l'Ecole Centrale de Paris, and graduated first in his class. He too had worked as an engineer in France and spoke the language perfectly. Later in life he would lead Egypt's government as prime minister and achieve the rank of Pasha, the only disappointment my mother had when she saw him was that he already was bald . . . and she had always dreamt of having a husband with a lot of hair that she could glide her hands through and fondly caress—in reality that was a minor detail, and she quickly overcame her disappointment. His mother, my grandmother, though of fierce intelligence, could neither read nor write and spoke only Arabic. Her father had been very rich, and she inherited much of his fortune. Arabic is a difficult language to master, and later during the years of Nasser, my lack of understanding of the national language was a handicap. As Egypt became more modern, I felt out of step with the rest of my country, as did many of my friends. This dichotomy was to lead to grave consequences for many of us.

Really, I lived my life in a rather adventurous way I did, almost in spite of my background. It should have been difficult for me to forgo all of it—the beneficence and grace of that cloistered life. And yet it was not.

5

CB

After an early childhood filled with gaiety and doting, pliable nannies, I was introduced to my stern British governess at the age of eight.

Miss Fanny Bodvan-Griffith was an albino, very tall and nearly blind, with translucent skin and pale, lashless eyes. A cultured woman from a rather good family, Miss Griffith spoke French and English, and had been a governess to the children of French noble families. Although I hated her on sight, and my sisters and I pleaded with my mother to "get rid of her, please!". Miss Griffith was to become perhaps the greatest influence of my life.

Mother ignored our complaints about our implacable new governess; I think she was ready to instill a new order of discipline in her cosseted daughters. At first, Doddy, Nini and I were dreadful to Miss Griffith, and the poor woman must have longed to be back with the well-born French children whom she had cared for before arriving in Cairo. I remember one of Doddy's early reactions to Miss Griffith's offer of tea at breakfast: she grabbed the cup and threw it at her. Miss Griffith marched Doddy to the bathroom, where she was to spend the next three hours. She emerged only somewhat chastened.

Doddy was always a little devil, and lazy about her studies and her musical practice. Yet she was immensely talented, and did well despite her lackadaisical ways. She would saw away on her little violin behind closed doors, pretending to practice while instead reading a book. Miss Griffith, normally so sharp, was none the wiser. Yet, when it came time to be graded on our music by a visiting Polish professor from the Warsaw conservatory, Doddy shone. I did well too, but only after practicing my piano assiduously, Miss Griffith looking over my shoulder.

After our warm and rather casual tutors, Miss Griffith was a blast of polar air. Now, I would stay seated at my desk until my homework assignment was complete; I would practice my piano for exactly one hour, not a minute less. No more rushing to the banister to peer down at every guest entering our hallway below; nor leaving the piano mid-scale to talk to my friends on the telephone. The new discipline improved my school grades—with regularity I began to achiever "Firsts" in my class.

After a few months of English lesson, Miss Griffith decided I was ready for the challenge of a new book, and she did not select a childish reader suitable for a nine-year-old. The book she chose for me was Dickens' David Copperfield. At first I rebelled: I couldn't possibly read that big book! But of course Miss Griffith would not countenance any weak-mindedness. It took me a very long time, but I got through that tome, and found that I loved every bit of it.

I became my father's favorite child, perhaps in part due to Miss Griffith's machinations. My governess was not fond of my mother, and she pushed me toward my father, the prime minister and Pasha of whom most people were afraid. Routinely Miss Griffith would stand me in front of my father to ask how I had done in my monthly class grading. Usually I could tell them both that I had achieved a "First", which meant that I had outshone all the other children in the class. When my father asked Doddy, she would proudly tell him she achieved a "Third". How many children in your class, he would ask; "three!" she would reply gaily. Doddy was four years older than I and my father would scold her for being less intelligent than her little sister. But she was a wonderful girl with a sweet and mischievous nature, and she never begrudged me my sterling grades.

Doddy and I were always close, and in many ways we led parallel lives—we married good men, lived well and for the most part happily. But my eldest sister Nini lived a difficult life from the day she was born, and it breaks my heart still.

My mother had ecclampsia giving birth to poor Nini, and spent several months in a semi-coma. Amidst the family's distress over my mother the baby was ignored by everyone, though she suffered with a lung ailment. Throughout her days, this bad luck would follow her.

CB

Miss Griffith lived with my family for many years, long after I had left the home to be married. Rather surprisingly, she chose not to return to England, which she said she would find boring after the excitement of Cairo. She was very adventurous, half-blind as she was, and loved walking through the city. She took her lunch and dinner—and often her much-loved glass of scotch—with my parents every day, to my father's quiet dismay. Later, as a prime minister during the Suez crisis, he saw his moment. Since Britain was now the enemy of his homeland, Miss Griffith must leave his home. My father, a highly moral man, could now move his children's retired governess from his house with a clear conscience. Because I was no longer living at home, I could not protest. Miss Griffith was given a generous monthly stipend, and set up in an apartment which I often came to visit. I think she was happy in her beloved adopted city, and she lived to a fine old age.

Miss Griffith's emphases on rigorous discipline and focus have become second nature to me, and have served me well throughout my life. Years later, my beloved nieces, daughters of Doddy, would tease me for being her long-ago favorite, "Doddy and Nini are *carrement bete*, "truly stupid". But Nevine! She is Miss Griffith's *chef d'oeuvre*! "Her masterpiece".

My parents' marriage was a happy one, though it surely had its difficult times. They led an active and complicated life. My father served as Egypt's undersecretary for public works and later became prime minister, and his wife was ideally suited to be a politician's wife. She loved entertaining and organizing, as I do, and she was extraordinarily social as well. There were parties at the palace, and visiting dignitaries to host. Her example was a fine one for me, and I was well-prepared for my first marriage to a diplomat. We lived in Paris and there was much entertaining and so forth. Because I had always seen it done so well by my mother, it was not a challenge to me as it might have been for other young wives. Many years later when my second husband, Bill, was transferred to London, my only job was that of a constant entertainer, and I loved it. I still adore having dinners and parties. I am known for my beautiful tables; I am meticulous. In fact, if I came back to this world I would like to return as a table dresser!

CHAPTER 2

In fact, now that I think of it, my childhood as exceptional as it was, was a very happy one. Everything went very well for me, I had wonderful parents who loved and cherished us, and left our upbringing and education almost entirely in the hands of Miss Griffith, whom they trusted implicitly.

Life was simple and easy and very disciplined. At age seven I was sent to the "e-cole Morin" to start my education. This French school was very near our house, started at 8:30 am and ended at 12:30 noon. It was located in Zamalek and we could see the Nile from all its windows, it was surrounded by a large garden where lots of sporting events took place. The owners and headmasters were a nice elderly French couple "Mr & Mme Morin" their two children, Jacqueline & Pierre, were also educated there. Most of our professors were French and excellent in their specialties.

I will never forget my first day at school in kindergarten . . . we were made to wear a navy blue uniform, and I was very frightened in my new surroundings, so much so that I felt the need to go to the bathroom at one point, but was too shy to ask . . . so I proceeded to hide behind the big blackboard and relieve myself right there. Of course it did not go unnoticed and I was punished by the teacher "Madame Moreno" and made to stand in the corner in front of all my classmates. This was my first day and I was truly ashamed and embarrassed. And my white underpants had turned to navy blue because of the incident. As time went on, of course, everything became easier, and from the very beginning I was anxious to excel and be better than all the other children in my class, so I proceeded to work very hard at it. We were taught to read and write in French and my school became a wonderful place for me to be for the next few years until the final exams of the baccalaureat and philosophy which I graduated from with honors . . . I also became very proud of the fact that I was the only one in my family who succeeded in all my exams, as my sisters never even reached the "Baccalaureat". Doddy got married at 16, and Nini failed at that exam, and never tried to pass it again.

The day I succeeded at my "Bac" was in June, it was very hot in Cairo and I was very tired and nervous when one of my professors called me to inform me of the good news . . . it was 3 o'clock in the afternoon when he called and I immediately ran to my father's room to tell him of my success. He had just awakened from his daily nap. "Daddy I have succeeded at my "Bac" with "mention Bien" and I am second in Egypt." He looked at me slightly scornful and said, "second, why not first?!?" It upset me so much that I ran out of his room and rushed to my own room crying pitifully. Of course, my mother heard me and came to calm me down and said, "Please don't cry, we will have a party for you, with all your friends tomorrow". That was her way of solving things. But that hurt never left me, and to this day I can hear my father's voice and scorn. He had been first all his life, and could not fathom that his favorite child was not like him. It certainly was a tough lesson for me to learn, but probably a useful one.

I enjoyed all these learning years immensely, and to this day I still am very grateful to have had such a thorough education. I do think that the French system of education is the best, though it is very tough. Once you get through it though you are well prepared for life and have acquired a tremendous amount of knowledge in most subjects.

I was in school from 1937 to 1947, all through the war years, and we were so lucky to still have all the wonderful professors who made us like and absorb all they were teaching. French literature, history, geography, etc. So by the time you graduated you were as educated as the French children and felt totally at ease in any French circles. So much so that my only wish was to continue at the Sorbonne.

When I asked my father to send me to Paris he said "no, you're only role in life is to get married and have children!" I wonder now what my father would think of me and the life I have lead, had he known then what I was about to decide to do with my life!

But let's not anticipate . . .

Those 10 years of schooling seem to have passed very rapidly and I thoroughly enjoyed them. They sure were probably the best part of my childhood. Many great events though happened during those years in our family to alter the course of our lives.

I guess the major event was the arrival in Egypt of our future King Farouk, coming from London where he was studying after the death of his father King Fouad in 1937. I will always remember seeing the carriage that led him through the streets of Cairo, looking so glamorous in his white military uniform. We had been lucky enough to have a special balcony in town where we were able to have a long glimpse of him . . . and it was a real thrill. The applause of the crowd in the streets was deafening and all his people seemed to really adore him. It is so sad to think how his popularity dwindled with the years and how his reign ended . . . but I don't want to get ahead of myself.

Cʒ

Before he became King, Farouk wanted to see his country, especially Upper Egypt which he had never been to and which to this day is the location of the most important pharaonic treasures. My father came home one day and told us that we were going to be following the king in a boat on the Nile, as my father then was undersecretary of state for public works, and one of his duties was to survey the Nile. It was going to be a 1 month long journey and he was sure we were going to enjoy it. Of course my sisters and I were very excited at the prospect of traveling, but the biggest attraction no doubt was to have an opportunity perhaps of meeting our future king. There were about 12 boats following the Royal vessel "the Mahroussa" (the blessed one) and our boat was almost the last one. All the boats sailing on the Nile were very comfortable; we had our private cabins and bathrooms, and wonderful living quarters. It is hard to imagine more beautiful scenery than the banks of the Nile. Nothing has changed really in 3000 years. The peace and serenity of it all is hard to fathom, as Romain Gary so well described it: "Le Nil est un lieu où l'âme se repose" (The Nile is a place where the soul is at rest). That is so true and so heartfelt.

For me to this day I get a tremendous thrill from sailing on the Nile. It remains one of the great joys of my life to have had the opportunity to have done it so many times.

So we started our journey from Cairo and every night we stopped in a different town or village along the way, as boats do not sail on the Nile at night. Our procession was greeted every evening by throngs of well-wishers who welcomed their future king with songs dances and fireworks . . . the festivities were non ending and the people really were anxious to welcome their future monarch.

Of course along the way we visited all the wonderful monuments and temples of ancient Egypt and we were lucky enough to listen to a great Egyptologist, the French "Abbé Drioton" who was enlightening Farouk with all his vast knowledge of pharaonic times. For me, only 8 years old, it was the first time that I started to understand what my country was about, or rather had been about, and it was fascinating. When you are a kid that age, you are like a sponge, everything you hear is like a revelation and the first impressions are everlasting.

This was indeed a great experience for me and I can never forget it.

CƷ

When we reached Assiout, half way from Cairo to Upper Egypt, my parents received a telegram informing them of my paternal grandfather's death in Cairo. My father had to ask permission of the future king to go back to Cairo for the funeral. Farouk told him not to worry about the children, he would look after them!

So he had our boat moored behind his every evening, and a covered gang plank joined the 2 boats. The future king (only 16 years old at the time) was then able to come and play with my sisters whenever he felt like it. They would have pillow fights and his future majesty would proceed to knock down every light bulb on our boat, just for fun and games.

We all had a lovely time and we looked forward every evening to his visits, and the games he invented and was anxious to play.

Luxor was the most amazing city of Upper Egypt with all its temples and tombs, and even at my young age I could understand what a great civilization Egypt had had at the time of the Pharaohs. The walls of the tombs were especially fascinating with all their writing in hieroglyphics, and all the vivid descriptions of life 3000 years ago. Quite unbelievable and astounding. It made me very proud to be Egyptian, and I also felt very lucky and spoiled to be leading such a wonderful life . . . almost like a fairy tale. Coming back to Cairo after such a super trip was somewhat of a letdown . . . but lots of events were happening around us.

Our future King decided that summer to go to Switzerland for a holiday with his mother and sisters, and as my mother's sister, aunt Zeinab was lady in waiting to the Queen mother, she was going on the trip and her daughter, my cousin Safinaz Zulficar was also invited to join them. My father that summer decided to take all of us to Europe for a couple of months, and one morning as we were in Chatel Guyon,

I woke up and told my mother I had had a very vivid dream. I dreamt I saw the King in my maternal grandmother's big hall in her house in Alexandria, and he was handing a box of "dragees" (sugar coated almonds), to my cousin Safinaz, who we always had called Fafette. My mother said to me "that's a very good sign". She no sooner had said it, that the hotel clerk where we were staying knocked at our door and delivered a telegram. "Fafette engaged to King Farouk". That was some news, and my dream now made more sense. My first cousin Fafette was to become Queen of Egypt! Wow!

☙

The Royal wedding was to be held in January 1938, and I had been asked to attend the ceremony as I was one of the 4 children summoned to carry Fafette's heavy train. It was so very exciting. The wedding took place in the Palace of Kubbeh where huge multicolored tents had been set in the beautiful tropical gardens. Before we came down to the gardens we were waiting in the Palace, the 4 kids holding and carrying the train, and the King in his white uniform and all his medals looked fabulous, so did Fafette who was now to be named Queen Farida. The king seemed a little nervous and at one point he pressed his 2 gloved hands together, and one of the gloves split and came undone. He immediately asked his entourage to bring him another pair of gloves. 2 minutes later, there were 6 more pairs of white gloves presented to him! At that point I thought, that's what it's all about to be King, you ask for 1 pair and are presented with 6 pairs. Wow!

We finally made it to the gardens and to the sumptuous dinner served to us on gold plates by the help wearing colorful red and gold uniforms. There were beautiful fireworks illuminating the skies of Cairo and cannons sounding in the background.

After dinner, the Queen mother distributed gold coins to all the guests and royal family to celebrate the occasion. The fairy tale had come true. My 2 sisters had not been invited to the wedding. I happened to be the right height and age to be one of the train bearers. That was certainly one evening that I have never forgotten.

King Farouk was very playful and imaginative and I remember one instance when I happened to be asleep at 9 o'clock at night in our house, when my mother came storming into my room to wake me up and say "hurry up and get dressed, the King has asked us to go with him to Alexandria right now".

I must have been 9 years old, and of course was delighted at having to get up and go to the Palace at night instead of sleeping! We arrived at the palace and the royal train was waiting to take us to Alexandria. It took about 3 hours to get there and when we arrived at midnight at Montazah palace the King had ordered taxi cabs, as he had never ridden in one, and wanted to have that new experience. There were about 12 of us in 2 cabs at midnight in Alexandria, and as usual the cabs were in bad shape and one of them broke down, so we all pulled into my grandmother's garage and the king started to drive her car for about 10 miles to get to his other palace of "Ras-el-Tin". By that time it was 2 o'clock in the morning, of course I was wide awake and enjoying every minute of it. It was all very thrilling!

As we arrived at the palace, a guard at the gate stopped us and the king shouted to him "Al Malek" (the King)! And of course the gates were immediately opened, and we proceeded to his majesty's huge boat where a lovely supper was awaiting us in the dining room. By that time it was almost 5am and there happened to be an upright piano in the dining room, and the king, having heard I knew how to play the piano, asked me to play! I could not refuse his royal command so I started to play Beethoven's Fur Elise as best I could, and they all applauded and I felt very grown up to be able to perform! We soon all went to bed and his majesty at 7:30am started to wake us all up by blowing into a trumpet outside our cabin doors. That was his way of having fun!

After that lovely weekend the king caught the measles and so did my eldest sister Nini, Doddy and I were spared as we had already had the measles. Now that I think of it, I can easily say that I had a very happy and even golden childhood. Wonderful doting parents, lots of lovely friends, and two loving sisters. I must have been blessed!

CB

Eventually the years went by rapidly, the Second World War started in 1939 and Egypt was almost invaded by the German troops. During that time my father was appointed prime minister of Egypt by King Farouk.

The German invasion was stopped at the Battle of El Alamein, and the war operations were after that mainly in Europe.

My father was pro allies, and King Farouk was pro German, which was hard to understand for all of us. We got accustomed to seeing lots of British soldiers in our streets, and actually almost took them for granted.

My father at that time had our house enlarged and almost all rebuilt, meanwhile we lived on a government boat on the Nile at walking distance from our house. That was a new experience for me, and I greatly enjoyed living on the river. We got accustomed to being awakened by the sirens announcing an air raid, and since there was no shelter on our boat we had to go to the shelter of Russell Pasha whose house happened to be across the street from our boat. Russell Pasha was a very nice English gentleman who was head of Cairo police at the time. It was all quite frightening but very exciting at the same time.

Life went on as usual though, my mother was very busy as she had founded the Red Crescent in Egypt (equivalent to the Red Cross) and had organized a team of Egyptian ladies who worked very hard at helping every way they could the refugees which flocked to Cairo coming from Alexandria which was much nearer to the Libyan desert and the war operations. Hoards of them came by train to the capital every day to escape the bombardments taking place near the Mediterranean coast line.

My mother being president of the ladies committee of the red \ crescent took her benevolent duties and job extremely seriously, and I used to tease her often saying to her "we never see you anymore, it seems to me we now have a brother called "crescent" that you prefer to your daughters"!

During the war years she was for sure a very busy lady, working very hard and doing an excellent job both at being a prime minister's wife with all its worldly obligations, and at the same time organizing and managing the Red Crescent.

In retrospect, I realize what a wonderful job she was able to do, and the amount of energy she spent in so doing. I have to say that I greatly admired her.

During those years my second sister Doddy got married to a wonderful man whom I loved dearly and became very fond of. Marriages in Egypt were most usually arranged marriages, it was the parents who really chose the 2 partners, and more often than not, they were very happy marriages, as parents usually made sound decisions based on facts unlike young people who tended to only think of love and happiness. So my future brother in law had expressed the wish to meet my eldest sister Nini in view of asking her hand in marriage. A tea party was therefore arranged for the 2 young people to meet at my cousin Loula's house. Low and behold he caught a glimpse of Doddy who was in the background making sandwiches for the occasion, and in no uncertain terms, told Loula, "it's not the eldest one I want to marry but the second one!!" Loula was shocked and told him "I cannot ask my uncle for his 2nd daughter to get married before the first, but my father was thank God, quite broadminded and said "that's fine with me" but I must ask the King's permission first.

At that time his majesty had commandeered a beautiful hotel, the "Winter Palace", in Luxor in Upper Egypt to spend a couple of weeks of R & R, and had invited our family to join him, Queen Farida, and all his family to spend the Holiday with them. We had a wonderful time.

The "Winter Palace" is a lovely hotel, which is still in operation today, all the rooms face the Nile, and it is surrounded by a very beautiful tropical garden. Se we all really "had a ball", I should say a

"Royal Ball", and when the King was asked his permission for Doddy to get married to Mahmoud, not only did he approve but named Mahmoud to a high job at his court.

Queen Nazli, the Queen mother was appalled saying, "You should never allow the 2nd daughter to be married before the eldest". But the King prevailed, and I will never forget our arrival that night at the train station in Cairo and Mahmoud with a bouquet of white roses in hand, and Doddy, half trembling and emotional stepping off the train and walking towards her new life and future husband!

Doddy was barely 16, and I was 12 at their wedding which turned out to be a fabulous affair, planned to perfection by my mother who loved nothing more than planning a party.

Cousin Queen Farida wedding to King Farouk.
Nevine Miller, age 8, far right.

CHAPTER 3

The celebration of weddings is very important in Egypt and calls for a tremendous amount of planning and organizing, as a lot of rituals have to be observed.

In our families specially, as on my mother's side we are half Turkish and I would say descendants of the Ottoman harems. I have previously described King Faruck's wedding celebration, 2 years later the Shah of Iran: Mohamed Reza Pahlavi came to Egypt to wed Princess Fawzia, sister of King Farouk.

I was asked to be a bridesmaid at that wedding also which was a grand event attended only by the Royal Family. All I recall from that time was the unbelievably beautiful amount of jewelry worn by all the princesses which literally dazzled my young eyes.

Of course it was very exciting at the age of 10 to be part of such glamorous events, but I was almost taking all of it for granted and in my stride.

My sister, Doddy's wedding took place in our house in Zamalek and was a splendid affair. There were in essence 3 wedding days of celebration.

The first being a tea party for men only about 60 of them, witnessed the signing of the contract between my father and the groom and a sheikh. The tea party was held in the adjoining garden, (The fence between the 2 gardens had been torn down). The King insisted to offer that party as a gift to my parents.

The second was a lavish spectacular soiree, when Doddy, only 16 wore a beautiful dress made by Vassel (the only couturier in Cairo at the time), and only the Royal Family attending as guests—roughly 160 guests.

There were 10 bridesmaids and 10 bridegrooms of more or less the same age and height. I was one of them of course, at 12 years old at the time I enjoyed every minute of it. The bridal procession coming down from the house to the garden was headed by a belly dancer and her band followed by us children, boys carrying huge lit candles, and girls a bouquet of white roses.

Then came Doddy (looking beautiful) in her long white gown and Mahmoud in his coat tails also very glamorous. At the same time as the signing of the contract, the ladies of the family stayed upstairs and the bride to be had to have her bare feet in a bucket of water in which flowers and gold coins were afloat. In one hand the bride held a lit candle and in the other a mirror . . . but the most important thing was that in her mouth there was a "dragée" (sugar coated almond). All this was symbolic of course and represented her future life to be always as flowing as water, with flowers and gold, she should look always as pretty as on her wedding day (as she could see in the mirror) and her path should always be lit. From now on every word she uttered should be as sweet as sugar!

All these rituals were mostly observed in Turkish families as they had come to Egypt at the time of Mohamed Ali and his Turkish harem. The third event was a repeat performance of the second in front of 800 guests, family, friends and diplomats.

Nini's wedding in 1942 was quite different, as the war was at our frontiers we could not decently have a big party.

Nini had gotten engaged to a prominent lawyer whom my father eventually appointed as his minister of the interior (which was probably a big mistake on his part).

The King and Queen though did attend the party, which was very dull, and towards midnight the King seemed bored out of his wits and demanded that we put records on the gramophone to lighten the atmosphere somewhat.

So some of us started to dance on our large terrace and the next day when I met our English neighbors "the Besleys" they said to me: "when we heard the music coming out at midnight from the prime minister's house, we knew that everything was going to be alright".

And in fact it eventually did turn out alright as the allies soon won the Battle of El Alamein, which was definitely a turning point of the war.

So, life went on, still very agreeably in Egypt, in spite of the war now raging in Europe.

The war ended in 1945, and that summer my father decided I was not to go to Alexandria to the seaside as usual, but he sent me to Lebanon for the summer with my governess and my sister Nini, her husband and their two babies.

His decision was prompted by the fact that he had received an anonymous letter from someone who claimed that his daughter Nevine was messing around with two young boys of her age who were cousins, and causing a lot of trouble between the two boys who were fighting for Nevine's attention.

So my father, old fashioned as he was, decided that the best way to stop all that nonsense was to avoid my going to Alexandria that summer, and sent me to Lebanon.

At first, of course, I did not like that decision at all, as in reality for the first time in my young life, I had fallen in love with one of the cousins.

That was my first experience of LOVE, and I must say it was quite enjoyable and real to me, though there was absolutely no sex involved, except for my first kiss which I cannot ever forget.

We stayed in the mountains of Lebanon for 2 months, and I enjoyed it, as my brother in law took us to Palestine for a week's tour which was very interesting . . . we visited all the sights, mosques & churches, and synagogues, but what I remember mostly is discovering a music shop where I could buy many classical music records which did not exist in Egypt at the time. I bought Beethoven's Emperior Concerto played by Rudolph Serkin, and listened to it so much when back in Cairo, as at that time music had become tremendously important to me, I had started to play the piano a lot and enjoyed it immensely.

That was my youth. Full of work, music, and love. Feelings that have remained with me throughout my life, and which have always been extremely important to me, and still are even at my age.

To sum it all up, I can earnestly say that I have always been a very active adult, my greatest passion has always been classical music and I have always been very lucky with all the love I have had in my life, and all the ones I have loved!

King Farouk and his bride and sisters at Doddi's wedding.

The Shah of Iran saluting my first cousin, Queen Farida of Egypt.

Royal Family with Shah of Iran, Princess Fawzia, sister of King Farouk.

Royal family at Shah of Iran's wedding.

CHAPTER 4

The 2nd World War ended in 1945 and everything started to fall back into place once again.

My childhood was over, and I remained for a few years as the only child in my parents' house. My 2 sisters were married and having babies, and I had finished my studies successfully, and of course, was still fretful about going to college in Paris and attending the Sorbonne but my father would hear nothing of it. So in 1947 he decided to spend the summer months in Europe instead of Alexandria, and took my mother and me to Vulpera/Tarasp in the mountains in Switzerland. He left us there to go to the U.S. on business. Meanwhile we spent 2 wonderful weeks in Lucerne where a fabulous music festival was taking place. My mother and I would go every evening to the concert where such great artists as Furtwängler and Dinu Lipatti were performing. For me it was a revelation, to finally listen to such great concerts, as music had become my true passion.

We ended our journey in Paris & stayed at the "California" hotel, rue de Berri. Having had all the French education I had had, Paris was the culmination of a dream, and far beyond my expectations. The sheer beauty of the city struck me and I proceeded to visit all the museums, galleries, monuments that I could manage . . . and had a wonderful time as well.

Some of my best friends from Egypt, the Ratibs, were also staying in a hotel nearby, and I spent many days with them having loads of fun. They all had been to Megeve for the summer and had also befriended a cousin of my mother's, Ismail Mazloum. Little did I know at the time, that my life would change entirely because of befriending Ismail.

We would spend quite some time together touring Paris, and one evening as we were waiting for the Ratibs' to join us for dinner near Montmartre at a cheese restaurant called Androuet, I told Ismail how lucky he was to be a student in this beautiful city as he was studying political science. He jokingly said "Well shy don't you marry me, we could have what the French call a "marriage blanc", and you also could stay in Paris". Of course, I took that as a joke, and soon returned to Egypt with my parents. Shortly after I started getting many letters from Ismail describing his life in Paris and all the lovely times he was having there.

A little before Christmas, his letters became much more pressing and after a while he proceeded to really ask me to marry him. Of course, I showed the letter to my parents, to see how they felt about it. They were a little surprised at first that it all had happened so fast, and told me that I had to make that decision.

As far as they were concerned Ismail had all the attributes of a perfect husband for their youngest daughter. He was from an excellent family, good looking, charming, had very rich parents, and also had the same kind of education and background as I had . . . so it was now all up to me to decide of my future. What a responsibility!

My parents left for Upper Egypt to spend Christmas with Abboud Pasha and his family who had a beautiful compound a few miles south of Luxor, which was utterly fantastic. Right on the Nile, with tennis courts, swimming pool, a stable of Arabian horses and all the amenities and luxuries that money can buy.

In December, Ismail came back to Chiro for the holidays, and I believe to see me also. I was very attracted to him, but hesitated somewhat to give him an answer. We would take long walks every day around the Guezira Sporting Club, and he would constantly press me further and demand an answer to his question.

He could not quite understand why I was hesitating. I could not either as I was gradually falling in love with him also.

I asked him to come one afternoon to our house in Zamalak, and told him that I would answer him then.

We sat quite a while in my parent's living room downstairs and I reluctantly told him what my hesitancy was about.

"I have heard a rumor about your liking boys", I said in a shaky voice, "and as I'd like everything to be clear and honest between us, I am just wondering if it's true". He looked at me with sadness in his eyes, and answered; "no, I do not like boys, and if I want to marry you it's because I have fallen in love with you, and I'd like to spend my life with you and have a family and children with you."

There were tears in his eyes, and I could see and feel how much I had hurt him. Plus I also had fallen in love with him and uttered in a very low voice; "yes, I will marry you, because I think I love you also."

And that was it.

We called my parents in Upper Egypt and told them the good news. They congratulated us and wished us "all the happiness in the world" then drank champagne to our health and happiness.

Our wedding was the most spectacular ever. Ismail came back to Cairo in March, I stood waiting anxiously for him in the Cairo airport. He had brought with him a huge carton with the name Christian Dior inscribed on it. Obviously it was my beautiful wedding dress coming from Paris and going through customs in Paris he was asked why he had a carton instead of a suit case. He answered "because I'm a poor student and a carton is less expensive than a suitcase!"

When my father got the bill for that dress he about had a heart attack, but he survived. Our wedding was a super affair, totally organized by my mother, as I was the last daughter, it had to be the best event ever. And it was!

On the 28th of March, 1948 we had the most beautiful soirée ever that started at 9 o'clock p.m. and ended at 5 a.m. when the last of the 800 guests left.

Somewhat a repetition of Doddy's wedding, but the King and Queen did not attend, as they were divorced by then. We had 8 bridesmaids & 8 bride's boys in the procession, preceded by the best belly dancer in Egypt, "Karioka" and her band. My dress was the most beautiful ever from one of Dior's first collections after the new look and we came down to the garden and sat on the "Kosha" and Karioka proceeded to dance the most erotic dances she knew how. Ismail nudged me and said "look & learn", as the belly dancer is there to supposedly put the newleyweds "in the mood" for what is to happen later.

A huge buffet of Egyptian specialties were served and Champaign flowed abundantly after the cutting of the multi-tiered cake we all danced to a jazz band on the terrace till the wee hours of the morning.

We had been given a huge amount of presents, they actually filled a room, and I had been very lucky as I received a great amount of jewelry, diamonds, emeralds, sapphires, etc, as Boucheon (a place Vendome Jeweler) had just had an exhibition in Cairo and all our friends had literally bought a lot of it specially to give as gifts for that occasion. When I think of it now, I realize how lucky I was at that young age to get so much attention, and be given so many precious and beautiful gifts to start my new life. And a new and wonderful life it sure was.

We spent a few nights in the Heliopolis Palace hotel to consummate our marriage and loved every minute of it. A few days later we went to Alexandria, accompanied by my parents and Abboud Pasha, president of the Khedivial mail line, to sail to Marseilles on our way towards our new surroundings in Paris, and our new life.

It certainly was a great and pleasant beginning. The sea was calm, and the boat huge and very comfortable, we had a lovely cabin & another one for all our luggage, all of it gifts from Abboud Pasha. 4 days later we landed at Marseilles where a strong mistral wind greeted us. Having had a lovely time on board, and also having met many lovely people as well.

We both were very happy and very much in love. We then boarded the night train to Paris, and were welcomed the next morning by Mr Gilbert Martin at the gare de Lyon. The Martins had a huge apartment at 284 Blvd St. Germain where Ismail, as a student, had been renting one room, and when he brought back his new bride, was able to secure a 2nd one & 1 bathroom.

It was quite exciting for me, and very comfortable. We had our meals with them & their 2 boys, and they were always delicious as Mrs. Martin was a superb cook. It suited me fine as I had no idea how to boil an egg even, and was very happy not to have to do any of the domestic chores which I had never had to do yet.

Paris of course was wonderful and we discovered its beauty and were fascinated by all the city of light had to offer us. We felt very lucky to be there at that time, even though the city was still recovering from the war. Food was still rationed & one could not get milk easily even . . . but that was a small price to pay for all we had instead, the theatre, the concerts, the galleries, the culture, and the sheer beauty of the city itself.

Nevine in her Christian Dior wedding dress.

Nevine and her husband sitting on the "KOSHA". March 28, 1948.

3 generations at the wedding.

Leaving on our honeymoon. Pictured with Abboud Pasha, owner of the Khedivial Line.

CHAPTER 5

Life in Paris

So it's in the 7th Arrondissement in Paris that our new life began. The apartment was very large and there was a grand piano in the living room, which I played on a lot, and so did my husband.

A few weeks later I started having morning sickness and immediately found out that I was pregnant. That was a real shock to me. I was only 18 years old, and not yet ready to have the responsibility of a baby. It was slightly frightening. Also, I felt terrible all the time, and that sure was no fun.

That summer we went to the mountains for our honeymoon which we really had never had. We went to "Cauterets" in the Pyrenees. I remember reading Dostoyevsky at the time and sometimes wondering how I had come to be there . . . but the time passed quickly. We took long walks in the mountains and loved each other a lot.

After Cauterets, we went back to civilization & landed in Biarritz in the Palace hotel where Doddy & Mahumoud joined us for a while, and we had lots of fun in spite of my morning sickness.

This is where for the first time I heard a budding singer called Edith Piaff who sang "LaVie en Rose" for the 1st time. That has remained my favorite song to this day . . . and I myself have sung it often.

We were back in Paris in the fall for Ismail to go to Science Po University. We decided to go back to Cairo for the birth of our child and stayed with my parents for 1 month prior to the birth. It was a girl and we named her Nimet, short for Nimetullah, i.e. "Bounty of God". We brought the baby to my in-laws house in Meadi, a lovely suburb of Cairo. My father in law had a room and a bathroom built on the 3rd floor of his house for the new baby.

We spent a few months there when my father had a brain wave and asked Ismail what were his plans for the future. And my husband answered that he wanted eventually to join the Egyptian diplomatic corps. So he took his exam for that and my father, then minister of foreign affairs, asked me where I wanted him to appoint my husband. I answered "Paris of course" and so it was! As easy as one, two, and three . . . we were real spoilt, but how nice that sure felt.

So off we went again to the City of Light, but this time with a job.

Our first concern was to find a flat which we were very lucky to find in the XVI Arrondissement at 50 rue Cortambert it was a huge apartment, 4 bedrooms, 3 bathrooms & study, living room with a grand piano, dining room, huge entrance hall, all beautifully furnished for the modest fee of $50/month . . . of course, we grabbed it. It belonged to a Countess de Boigne, who was utterly charming, and slightly afraid of renting to Egyptians.

She never was sorry though because Ismail proceeded to redo the apartment & have every room reupholstered making it very much nicer. We spent 4 years in Paris and they were wonderful years. We both enjoyed the same things, and had the same education and culture, so we felt quite at home in this beautiful city. Plus we had loads of money to spend, so our life was very easy, we had a cook, two maids and a Swiss nanny for the baby. It could not have been better or easier.

We also had many friends and became also the best friends of a couple that we got along with extremely well. She was an ex princess of Egypt who had divorced her prince and married an Albanian gentleman: Mahiveche Iskander De Villa. We ended up having a wonderful time with them as they loved the same things as we did so we traveled the country side often and spent our summers with them in the Carlton in Cannes.

What a life!

Mahiveche was the cousin of Fatma who had married Don Juan d'Orleans Bragance, brother of the Countess de Paris and most charming and simple . . . They also came to the Cote dázur and as they knew everyone, we had a ball with them.

Every day & night there was a different party either in big estates, or on lovely yachts and we tagged along always. What a life!

We really had great fun, and no worries at all.

CHAPTER 6

One of the great events that happened to me personally when we lived in Paris is the following.

On November 26th, 1951 our ambassador Ahmed Saroit being a bachelor, decided to have a huge party for all the delegates that were in Paris at the time for the United Nations Assembly. All the ladies married to the men working in the embassy were asked to organize it all and also to act as hostesses during the party.

After dinner I was standing with a few guests talking, when I noticed an old man with a beard coming towards us. He came and stood by my side and talked to me of various subjects and soon we were on a different plane speaking philosophy & religion. There was instant understanding between us.

I learnt later that he was the Minister of Foreign Affairs of Pakistan Sir Zafrullah **Khan**, and 2 days later he called me to invite Ismail & me to dinner at the "Tour d'Argent". The dinner went very well, of course because I did not dare to have wine as it is strictly forbidden by the Muslem religion, and Zafrullah was a fervent Muslim almost a mystic apart from that the dinner was absolutely delicious. We all had their famous duck, and answered all of Zafrullah's numerous questions as he prodded a lot to find out what kind of persons we both were.

A week later, having learnt that I loved music, he invited us to the Salle Pleyel to listen to Handel's Messiah.

He sat me near him near the front and Ismail sat at the back with the Pakistani Chargé d'Affaires. During the interval he handed me a letter. Supposedly it was the problem of a friend of his. He asked me to solve it and to answer it. I eventually received, in the next 10 years, around 400 letters. The first one was the most extraordinary one. It reads as follows:

November 26, 1951

You know how reluctant I was to come to Paris. I feel lonely and sad among seemingly joyous crowds. This appearance of joy is too often only a mask to cover up the stagnation of the mind and the bankruptcy of the soul. I had, however, a very pleasing experience this evening.

I was bidden to dinner where a large number of people were expected. My distressing habit of punctuality made me almost the first arrival. After greeting the host and bowing to the other members of the house party I passed on to seek some obscure corner in which to bury myself during

the greater part of the evening. I was conscious of having received a pleasant impression but did not care to analyze it or to search for its origin and was glad to have escaped into the emptiness of the vast salon.

Presently the sensation was revived but was somewhat confused. The room began to fill and my attention was claimed by a succession of people whom I knew. A slightly troubled feeling remained.

The meal over, I began to look for my companions so that we could leave. You are aware of the routine I tried to follow. When I found my companions they plainly intimated they desired to stay longer. I had now walked straight into the orbit of the planet. My instinctive reaction was to withdraw as if seeking shelter. You have often remonstrated with me on what you call my brusqueness and aggressiveness in similar situations. I am afraid I was again guilty. Yet I began to be surprised and then to be gratified with the persistent and increasing graciousness that appeared determined to compel the homage due. I resisted and diverted the conversation into graver channels as if by way of challenge. The Lady (who had been seated) rose to her feet with lithe and animated grace and with a gleaming smile intimated acceptance of the challenge. There was instant understanding.

I ceased to be troubled. My being felt suffused with a glow of joy. My state of mind was compounded of many sensations, the dominant one being relief. Here was no society sinner manipulating her charms to feed her vanity. That there was great charm was patent. She was too intelligent to be unaware of it. But she accepted it and carried it as she accepted the fact of being alive and performed the act of breathing. It was an inseparable and indispensable part of her being. There was no need to call it into play and to exercise it. Nor did she seek to employ any artificial modesty as a guard. Her transparent innocence was both her guardian and her champion. It appeared to cast a halo around her.

I had scarcely carried out the inner adjustment that this revelation entailed before she had moved away on an errand of courteous solicitude. To linger would have been to spoil perfection, so rarely achieved in life. I left.

Does this surprise you? You have often taxed me with demanding the impossible. All impossibilities have here combined to produce the <u>one</u> reality. The lady is a wife and mother and very grace itself.

November 30

My experience was no airy dream. The recollection has not been in the least dimmed by the hard realities of the day's work and worries. The harder the work and the deeper the worries, the greater the eagerness with which a delicate perfume, is hauntingly refreshing. In my mind there is no sense of strangeness. There is a feeling of comfort, of being understood, of having found comprehension. We exchanged but an observation or two. What mattered and is of value to me is not so much what was said but a realization of the fact of her being. That she is a mortal being of flesh and blood is not a fact to be taken for granted but a wonder and a mystery that exalts and uplifts. The astonishing thing is that there is on my side a calm acceptance of this flow of happiness. You have had occasion to warn me against my intensiveness which you say sometimes wearies even my close friends, an impetuosity that needs to be restrained. I do not in this case seem to suffer from it. The case is like the air we breathe; a vital necessity, an imperceived and yet a miraculous wonder, but not a matter of envy, jealousy or impetuosity. (The thought strikes one that it is a matter of complete indifference to the air weather one inhales it or not! Yet one may neglect the inhaling only at the risk of forfeiting the chance of ever being able to inhale again!)

Any intense reality is apt to obtain a poignant grip over the heart. One meets so many women. To most one's reaction is one of cold indifference, to some of active aversion: few make a pleasing impression. Then chance or accident brings one up face to face with one charged with the intensity of reality and the universe-embracing miracle is achieved. She too is a woman. There are many that bear a resemblance to her, yet she stands apart, unique. She combines in herself the gleam of the stars, the glory of the morning, the fragrance of the flowers, the colours of the rainbow and all the joy and sadness of the universe. The soul leaps to the recognition in her of its complement and counterpart. To know that she exists is to be filled with hope, to find her is to live, to be vouchsafed a glance is to be endowed with riches, to win a smile is to glimpse paradise, to be understood is Happiness itself. To desire more would be to seek to make that captive which can survive only in freedom, to attempt to make that finite which is infinite and eternal.

Here all seems well with her. She is at the threshold of a life whose enchanting vistas beckon and invite exploration with rich promises of joy and happiness. Yet she seems to know that no life is all joy. Sorrows may be encountered: pain may have to be endured. She will meet all with calm dignity. Her being is rooted in the verities of life.

Now there is the prospect of a meeting. I have not sought it, but nothing would be more welcome. It would not be a chance encounter. It is something granted: a bounty, a gift. I look forward to the occasion with eagerness but also with a little apprehension. I do not feel too sure of myself. The normal social courtesies should be easy. I have informed myself of the background so that I should not make a slip out of ignorance. But the background is only incidental, the personality is the reality. I am too intensely conscious of it. I am afraid of falling into gaucheries for fear of letting my appreciation become too obvious or too oppressive. As nothing is, however, likely to be gained by indulging in apprehension I must try to put it aside in the hope that everything will turn out for the best. I look forward to the promised joy in a mood of restrained impatience.

December 2

The great, truly great, event has happened. My eagerness but also has my apprehension were justified. I slipped unconsciously into an attitude of (I hope affectionate) intimacy which our previous slight contact had perhaps not warranted. I must have been nervous and in my effort to appear at ease I fell sometimes into banter. On the other hand I could not altogether avoid being abrupt or even brusque, a fault I am so much liable to.

But the eagerness suffered no disappointment. From first to last the evening (only too short) was an uninterrupted succession of wonders and agreeable surprises. I had (as far as it was possible) tried to put my mind in a completely unbiased state. At the very first moment it switched over to ecstasy. My first impression was not only confirmed and deepened, it was proved incomplete in many respects. The most agreeable experience was that of the utter graciousness, without the least trace of effort or design. That is a quality that one expects to find, in some degree, in all women of breeding. What was here most gratifying was the simple naturalness and the complete absence of any artificiality. It bore witness to a sense of justified self-confidence and was a charming tribute to and disarming trust in the company. This allied with youth and transcendent charm make the combination superb and unique. Had I not known she was of the East, it might have become difficult to accept the evidence of my eyes, ears and mind. This knowledge helped both to explain and to interpret. I perceived I had ceased to be astonished. There was a glow of satisfaction, of pride, of exultation born of a realization that all this emanated from a being who was in a very real sense one's own and that it was, therefore, not a matter for wonder, but something to be prized and cherished.

Can you imagine the deep and abiding joy of that realization?

I have come away completely happy, except for the consciousness of my own defaults and inadequacy. My mind revels in joy and overflows with gratitude to the Maker and that which He has made. This product of the Divine Creator's art is exquisite in respect of the harmony of its beauties and qualities. While this symphony was in progress I failed to detect a single discord, the faintest echo of a false note.

Yes, do believe this comes from me. I remember how often you have told me I am hard to please. You may recall someone's observation: "Not only do you not suffer fools gladly, you do not suffer gladly people even of moderate intelligence." I affirm here is a combination of charm and intellect that compels admiration, homage, devotion, adoration.

Am I in love? NO, not in any aspect of the accepted connotations of that expression. That would be sacrilege. But the Truth is that I Love completely and in the absolute. The poet has sung: "My heart leaps up when I behold a rainbow in the sky". My heart has leapt and danced with joy ever since I have been vouchsafed a glimpse of this exquisite rainbow penciled across the sky of life itself by the Divine hand of the Master.

I can express my appreciation, pay my homage, convey my gratitude only through my heart's devotion and adoration. If this be love, there is nothing more sacred in life than love: if this be not love, I know not what love may be. It seems to me this is the only true currency: the rest is counterfeit.

January 9th, 1952

Dt Nevine,

Yesterday, like several of its predecessors, opened foggy, but during the early afternoon the fog cleared and a pale wintery sun made its wan appearance. The evening came clear and clouded with a bright moon casting its witchery over sky and earth. The sight intensified the loneliness and emphasized the melancholy.

I received a letter from my cousin who has lately arrived in Geneve urging a visit. It occurs to me that if you are likely to cut your stay at Megeve short I might aim at arranging my visit to Geneve for Jan: 18-21. Before coming to a decision I shall, of course, wait for your suggestion. It also looks as if the Assembly Session might conclude earlier than was anticipated. It might, therefore, be wise to hold our reception a day or two earlier, for instance on Feb 4. What would you advise? I have not heard much more about the venue of the next Session. It appears that the South American delegations are divided, some suggest Paris and some Rio de Janeiro. The majority of the other Delegations would wish to remain in New York, but the Presidential election may be made the excuse for keeping out of New York at the time. There is also a suggestion to meet in New York but after the election. The decision may, in the end, veer round to Paris.

It has been raining here this morning. This may clear the fog and the air services which have been thrown completely out of schedule during the last three days may get back into their schedules.

I tried to call Ismail over the phone last evening to suggest we may dine together here this evening, but he had not yet got back from the Embassy. I shall try again after breakfast so as to catch him before he goes out.

You are sure to have reflected that in the nature of things we shall have very few opportunities of meeting. Even the communion of the spirit, so long as the spirit is wedded to the body and can only express itself through physical means, is dependent upon opportunities of expression through conversation and correspondence. These must remain limited. But such as they are they should be availed of to the utmost for the purpose of laying down the firm foundations of spiritual affinity and fellowship. (I am assuming, of course, that your need of such fellowship is as urgent as mine. I have no <u>reason</u> to make this assumption: but somehow I feel that I am being neither vain nor impertinent in making it. Am I right, Nevine? In the absence of such affinity all companionship and friendship, however long it might endure by mere computation of time, remains conventional. Even as such it has or, at least, may have great value and may fill urgent human needs. It certainly makes life pleasanter and the burdens of life much easier to bear. But it has no comparison with the communion and companionship of the soul. In this wholly sabaristic and materialistic life spiritual values have ceased to have much significance. It is very very much worthwhile to restore them to their proper place in the scheme of things in the Universe, and one can make a beginning in our own individual lives. God has made ample provision for the filling of that need as for all others. I have provided you with some of the material. I trust you will be able to spare a little time to study and reflect upon these matters. The paper on Religion sets out some of the fundamentals.

Am I being a nuisance, Nevine? Mind, <u>only</u> the truth!

God's Grace and Blessings unfold you every moment.

W.F.L. Y.

Z.

P.S. Ismail says he cannot dine with me this evening. He is dining with <u>friends</u>! But he has told me of your phone message that you are having plenty of sun. Good.

January 13th, 1952

Dt Nevine,

Just when my letter of this morning was going to the post I received from Paris your letters of Jan 8 and 9. I made a hurried note at the end of my letter that your letters had reached me. I trust you did not think that it was too curt. My reaction, as usual, was one of great joy; only there was no time (or space) to add anything more. By this time, I hope, you know me well enough to realize what a letter from you means to me. (Do you?). I hope, therefore, there was no risk of any misunderstanding.

NO, I was not in the least shocked by your second letter. As my convocation Address implies most people are in that position. Few have the courage or the honesty to acknowledge it to themselves, let alone to confess it to another. But that does not mean that the problem does not exist. As you have said the problem is too "vast and complex" to be discussed within the space of a letter. Besides treatment of a subject like this in a letter suffers from the drawback that one may proceed to expound a thesis which may be utterly irrelevant. In oral discussion it is easier to keep to the vital point. But will you be <u>able</u> and <u>willing</u> to spare the time? The problem is well worth devoting your time and attention to? Indeed it is the most vital problem in one's life. Let this be made clear at the outset. Each of us has to work out his or her own solution of it. Of course, study and discussion are helpful and often a single phrase or expression may bring a flash of understanding, but the solution and the satisfaction must come from oneself. That it <u>can</u> come is certain. That it <u>will</u> come depends upon the sincerity, earthnestness and perseverance that a seeker brings into his search. You may trust me so far as to accept from me the assurance that no other investment of one's time and faculties is so richly and extravagantly rewarding as this one.

I can, to some degree, appreciate your feeling of baffled frustration over these matters. The current presentation of them is too mechanical, is not a mere repetition at stated intervals of a set of prayers, is <u>not</u> a mere starvation for a period to be followed by indulgence. Till the true significance of these matters is realized they are apt to appear to one in the guise of penances constituting a discipline repellent to the soul and wearying to the body. The essence must first be grasped and realized. There is no mystery about it. It is easy to perceive if one is honest with oneself, out of the material that you already have to study you should (now that you have read through my Convocation Address) first read carefully "Why I believe in Islam", then once more very carefully "My faith" and then proceed with a study of "Ahmadiyyat, or the True Islam". "Introduction to the Holy Quran" you may continue all the time through that is more historical and explanatory. I shall, of course, assist all the time as far as I am able. But the principal means is prayer, earnest humble, yearning and constant. He who has planted in our souls the thirst and then yearning has also provided the fulfillment. Be very, very sure of that.

January 14th

NO, I have not surprised you into a rash promise. If you should have any suspicion of that, you are free to reconsider the matter. I had pondered over the matter for both of us before I put it you. I wanted to make the promise. Even the sense of shock has fulfilled its purpose. Your thoughts and mental processes have been propelled in the right direction. But you are free of the promise. NO companionship in Eternity can be based on constraint. If righteous souls yearn for each other's companionship they shall be vouchsafed their desire. This is a Devine Promise. NO further guarantee is needed. If our souls grow into comradeship here they will not be separated hereafter. If they drift apart here, they will neither desire nor seek each other in the Beyond. In the first case there will be no need to ask? One will wait for the other and will be there to greet its comrade and counterpart. It may even be appointed to conduct its twin half over unfamiliar places. That is as God's Mercy may determine. "A holy Brotherhood" the Quran calls such comrades.

This has become a solemn letter: but life, deep down, is a solemn affair. Did you not receive that impression in the very first moment of our meeting, Nevine? Yet, life is richly joyful too: only our standards are often at fault and we sometimes let our tastes become vitiated. But be not anxious and have no fear. You have the sincerity and the courage and the truth (the verities) that will see you through to a triumphant fulfillment.

When Ismail came to deliver the parcel he told me he could not leave Paris before the 25th, as the Foreign Minister was to be in Paris till them. I shall probably go to Geneva on the 18th but will confirm from Paris.

In God's keeping always.

W.F.L. Y.

Z.

Le 14 Jan (II)

Dt Nevine,

The journey from London was quite comfortable and we arrived at Le Bourget a quarter an hour ahead of time. You can imagine how impatient I was to get to the Hotel. My impatience was rewarded richly. I found your two letters (of Jan: 10 and 11) among my mail. My very grateful thanks, madonna.

First, as regards my visit to Geneve. I am planning to go there (as I said in my letter of this morning from London) on the afternoon of the 18th. I should be able to settle my programme definitely tomorrow and shall confirm it in tomorrow's letter. The best plan would be for me to call you on the phone from Geneva after arrival there and to settle details for your visit next day. I am more than delighted to learn you will be able to get down. We can discuss a number of subjects and a meeting will to me be, as you know, in any case, a great joy. The reception is being arranged for Feb 4, I am very glad to learn the mountain air is doing its work so well. You have already started gathering roses. I hope you will be able to bring a whole cluster down to Geneve and later to Paris and that they will last!

Relating to the alternation of sunshine and snow at Megeve I have been reminded of a few lines that a very dear friend wrote to me 40 years ago (dear me, how time flies) when we had a temporary misunderstanding. It was entirely my fault he was not in the least to blame, but we both suffered. This is how he said he tried to comfort himself.

> *Be still sad heart, and cease repining,*
> *Behind the clouds is the sun still shining,*
> *Thy fate is the common fate of all,*
> *Into each life some rain must fall;*
> *Some days must be dark and dreary.*

I do hope the weather improved after the 11th and that you were able to get some more exercise.

Have you noticed how often our minds run on the same lines? You ask me a question and by the time your letter gets to me I have already answered it in one of my letters, it has sometimes happened the other way also your letter of the 11th has anticipated some of the things I wanted to say to you and your mind has already grasped them and made them your own. From your letter of the 9th (to which I sent a reply in my letter of today from London) I had feared that your progress along certain lines might take longer than I could have wished and I was haunted by a sense of apprehension whether I would be granted enough time to see its full consummation. Then I rebuked myself at the vanity of the thought. So long as the Grace of god guided you along, what difference would it make how much of a share had been granted to me in the process? But God is vastly more Gracious and Beneficient than our puny and limited fancies can conceive. All praise be to Him. Your letter of the 11th shows you are already making rapid progress and that God goes on illumining your path Himself. Can you imagine what joy that realization has brought to me? The two letters have been written only two days apart, and yet they may have been written by two different persons, so greatly is the outlook already changed!

Continue your search earnestly, sincerely and seeking help and guidance constantly from Him Whom you seek and He will show you the way and guide you along it. It is only then that you will begin to learn the true meaning and significance of life, its true worth, its majestic dignity, the lofty achievements and its rich, pure and rare joys.

May all this be yours in rich abundance. Amen!

Have you had some conception of the urge behind my asking you for "the pledge"? Do you now realize a little better the significance of "a little, perhaps a very little, here, and the whole of Eternity?" Should God in His Mercy make us comrades in the spirit I shall continue to live through a part of my personality here even when the soul having quitted this narrow habitation of the body has been summoned into God's greater Grace and Mercy, and you will long before you arrive on the other side, have some foretaste of what your twin soul experiences of that Grace and Mercy. And when in God's good time we meet again. What perfect understanding, what perfect joy, what pure happiness, what a glorious reunion that will be! Do you still doubt that a siracle was worked about 10.30 p.m. on Monday, November 26th?

"I am grateful to you for having taken the trouble to try and put me on the way". Trouble, Nevine? It is joy supreme. May God accept it of us and bring the fruit thereof in its fullness for both of us. Amen.

We corresponded assiduously for several years and we saw each other at different periods either in Paris, Cairo, the South of France, etc.

After this first amazing letter he wrote me every day for the next few months, and gradually tried very hard to influence me in understanding and practicing my religion. i.e. Islam.

In January of that year, he also asked me if I would agree to spend my eternity with him, as he said that it was a divine promise that "if righteous souls yearn for each other's companionship they shall be vouchsafed their desire".

It took 3 letters on my part to tell him as nicely as I could, that I could not make that pledge, as I had my whole life to live to start with.

Above are 2 letters of January 13th & 14th 1952, trying, in his words, to convince me of his faith, and to acknowledge the "pledge" of spending my eternity with him.

He married a young Palestinian girl, whom I had met in 1958 when Zafarullah was judge at the international court of The Hague.

I had lunch with them both at their apartment in the Hague, and found it quite odd to see him with that very young girl . . . but I was happy for him and thought that maybe he had found in her his soul mate!?!

The last time I saw him was in New York in 1966, he came for dinner at my apartment and as usual we had wonderful conversations on various subjects.

In 1978 I called him in London, he was living there in the mosque in London, when I asked to see him, he told me he had retired from the world, and was not seeing anyone anymore.

On the whole our relationship had been a very extraordinary one, I never as much as touched his hand during all these years . . . and yet reading his 400 letters was a fantastic experience for me. Now that I am 83 years old, I realize all this happened some 60 years ago, but it remains very vivid in my memory.

May God bless you Zafrullah.

Foreign Minister Sir Zafrullah Khan with Eleanor Roosevelt.

Foreign Minister Sir Zafrullah Kahn with
Edwin A. Plitt of the U.S. Delegation.

CHAPTER 7

We spent 4 wonderful years in Paris enjoying every minute of it. We now had 2 children Nimet & Nihal, and indeed a beautiful life to show for it.

Actually, it was too good to be true.

A few events happened there that made me start to believe that my husband had probably lied to me when I accepted to marry him.

I started to suspect that his latent homosexuality was starting up again, and I tried very hard to fight it. He himself also, I have to recognize, tried also to fight it, because deep down he did love me.

It is quite difficult to fight another woman, but try fighting a man is almost impossible, one is not on one's own ground, and most likely one cannot win.

So I myself started to be quite miserable and he became very selfish and self-absorbed, and gradually gave in to his sexuality, which created a huge hurt in me, and made me less confident about myself. I felt that, as a woman, I had failed completely, and that sure was not a nice feeling.

In July 1952 our country suffered a great change. General Naguib and Gamal Abdel Nasser fomented a coup d'etat, and from one day to another ousted King Farouk who abdicated his throne and left in exile for Italy with his 2nd wife and children.

Our lives were changed forever.

One of the first decrees Nasser made was an "Agrarian reform" reducing a family's ownership to 300 feddans (300 acres) which was reducing the income of all the rich families tremendously.

A few months later another decree hit us directly, as all the diplomats who were in good posts like Paris, London, Washington were transferred to the worst posts ever. We were sent to Yemen.

Thank God we never made it there, but thanks to a little clout that my father still had, we were able to remain in Cairo and Ismail then worked at the foreign affairs ministry in Cairo.

Our last days in Paris, I can never forget. I was 23 years old then, my husband was having an affair with a Frenchman, and I had to make every decision by myself, because the 2 of us hardly spoke to each other anymore.

I decided to leave part of my jewelry in a bank in Switzerland, not knowing what the future held for us in "Cairo.

I also left some good furniture with some friends in Paris, sold our car, sent my children home with their nanny to Cairo, and carried all by myself all the weight of this great life change.

It was all a very heavy task, but I assumed it, and it probably made me feel very much responsible for all my little family, and capable of doing it all, while my husband could not have cared less, so involved was he at rediscovering his newfound sex life.

We sailed back to Alexandria, and on board things became slightly better between us but after all the turmoil, I felt I could never trust my husband again. And I was right . . . life was never the same as it had been in the first years of our marriage.

As we had nowhere to live we started by spending a few months at my in-laws in Meadi, and one day my father in law noticed that the 10 carat diamond ring I had on my finger which was my wedding ring, looked dirty and needed cleaning badly.

I proceeded the next day to take it to Pohoomull Jewelers, and asked them to have it cleaned.

The jeweler looked at it and said: "We don't need to clean it because it's not a diamond, it's a zircon". Of course, that was not good news for me as we were never able to leave Egypt for a few years after that incident—and in any case, I never had any proof as to who had changed my 10 carat diamond!

Unfortunately, incidents like this one do happen in one's life!

The post revolution years in Egypt were quite strenuous for us all, our friends and most of the people we knew. Nasser was now in full power and exercised his power to supposedly equalize the wealth of the people of Egypt. Take from the rich and give to the poor, so all our "class" (and I hate this word) was hit badly. From one day to another, for instance, my eldest sister and her husband were bereft of everything.

All their money in the bank was taken by the government, their lands sequestrated and suddenly my mother had to give them a monthly stipend to keep them afloat. And like them a great number of wealthy families were suddenly left penniless. Some of our friends were also put in jail, and life in our beautiful peaceful country became slightly unbearable.

And Nasser was leaning toward Russia to build his famous Aswan dam, as the U.S. and Foster Dulles refused to give us any help.

We all felt we were slowly going to become a totally socialistic country and even perhaps a communist one.

There was of course a feeling of stress and panic among the intelligentzia, and a lot of the ex-wealthy families were struggling to find a way of emigrating to more clement lands.

I, for one, had always wanted since age 15, to live abroad. Having been brought up the European way, and been taught to say "Nos Ancetres les Gaulois" (Our Ancestors the Gauls). I felt much more French than Egyptian—so much so that seeing the exodus around us of a lot of our friends, and of course a lot of Jewish people, and Europeans, there was a feeling of abandonment for those of us who were forced to stay in Egypt

In 1956, Nasser nationalized the Suez Canal which was previously under foreign rule, and a coalition of French, English & Jews proceeded to declare war to Egypt and tried to invade our territories.

We had very mixed feelings at the time, in one way we did not want our country to be invaded, and in another we hoped it would be because it would bring down Nasser's domination. These were serious and painful times for all of us, but the war came to an end pretty soon, and Nasser was able to celebrate his so called victory as the Suez Canal, an important thoroughfare for all those countries, was now under Egyptian control.

Meanwhile life went on in Egypt for us, my husband decided to retire from the Egyptian diplomatic corps, and soon after he and I decided to go into business for ourselves. There happened to be a fashion boutique called "La Grande Demoiselle" in town for sale, and we bought it. I told my father what we had done, and that I was going to join the work force, as the shop was put in my name, and I wondered if he minded my decision. He replied "il n'y a pas de sot métier, il n'ya que de sottes gens" i.e. "There are no stupid jobs, there are only stupid people". My husband told me then "you don't have to work at this shop we only have to put it in your name" . . . Well this was 1957, and I have never stopped working at various jobs from then until now!

We then started something which we knew not too much about, so much so that every month we had to pay our employees I would have to sell one of my jewels to meet the payroll.

At the same time, the fact that the daughter of a Pasha had joined the workforce was noticed by the powers that be, it was written in all the papers as a real news item, and somewhat approved by the new regime.

Another important event happened in my life, which left me very perplexed, but also very happy.

One day I was having a chat with my best girlfriend in Cairo, Tania, who asked me point blank if there was anyone in Egypt who had ever appealed to me. At first I said no, but upon reflection I said "yes, as a matter of fact, only one man that I have always admired a lot M.S., but somehow we have never had the opportunity of seeing each other that much." He was one of the big Pashas of Cairo, married of course, also one of the important men in Cairo, 20 years my senior, but charming and fun at the same time and with a great sense of humor.

So what I said to Tania, it did not fall on a deaf ear. A Couple of weeks later she called me (she lived in the same building as we did and so did my mother). She said she was having a few people for bridge that day, and she had invited my mother and M.S. (who was a champion bridge player) but was not inviting me!

Of course I told her in no uncertain terms what I thought of her, and she laughed and said "of course I'm inviting you also".

Tania was a Russian Princess Nahitchevanskii married to an Egyptian and a beautiful & charming lady, and also a wonderful friend. So, of course, I accepted her invitation, especially that at that time I was not even speaking to my husband, having discovered for sure that he was gay.

The evening went "aescendo" from start to finish, Tania had her Russian uncle passing through Cairo, and had invited just a few friends to meet him and play bridge. After a few hours of cards, she decided we should all go to the big house of a friend Mohamed Faizi, his house was facing the Nile and quite beautiful. There we all drank lots of vodka, and all of us started to sing Russian songs. The mood was very high indeed. And great fun!

A couple of hours later we went back to her house for dinner, and after dinner, I was sitting alone in the entrance hall which was quite dark, and after a few minutes M.S. came to sit next to me. Of course, my heart beat faster and before I knew it, he took me in his arms and kissed me!

The next day I went to my sister Doddy's house and told her about it, and she told me pragmatically: "So what, you'll have one lover in Cairo" Well, little did I know at the time what would happen, but as time went by I saw lots of M.S. he had left his wife and children in Paris, because that year 1961, was when Nasser proceeded to sequestrate and confiscate many of the wealthy Egyptians, and of course, M.S. was one of the prominent ones.

At the start of our fabulous love affair, M.S. asked me to consummate our relationship and I answered NO, saying to him, "I can't as I am in love with someone in New York, and that's it"!

Well from then on M.S. and I saw each other every day, and went out together every night to all of the Cairo restaurants and night clubs specifically to a boat on the Nile, where we used to stay till 3 am sometimes, completely immersed in our growing love.

All of Cairo society of course, thought we were lovers! Unfortunately, we were not, but I must say I started to dream of nothing else.

Eventually, after 6 months of that regime, M.S. told me one day, "enough is enough", you have to come to my house tomorrow at 6pm. I'll send the servants away, and you can park your car in my garage, next to my Rolls Royce". I said I would

So I went to M.S's house (it was all decorated by Jantzen, and most beautiful) I climbed the stairs immediately full of expectation and joyous anticipation.

We had a couple of drinks in his den after which he looked at me with sad eyes and said: "I cannot do anything here, there are too many pictures on the walls of my wife and children, I can't"! I answered: "I have the key to an apartment where we can go, it's far away, next to the Cairo airport, let's go!"

He acquiesced, and we left his house, me driving and he sitting next to me.

After ½ hour of driving during which I kept talking to him and saying, this is all so ridiculous, why did we not stay at your house? I looked at him, and he said: "I'm not feeling well at all". I knew he had already had 2 heart attacks, so I said "I'll take you home immediately, which I did. When we got there he asked me not to leave him alone, and to come up with him which I did.

He went straight to his bedroom, and put on his pajamas, and got into bed. A few minutes later he asked me to get into bed also, which I did.

He kissed me, caressed me and I looked at him, his face was red as can be, and he looked terrible. So I got out of bed, dressed and called "Aldo" his butler, and asked him to call M.S.'s doctor at once, because I was leaving. 2 hours later M.S. called me and said the doctor said he was having a heart attack, and if we had done what we were planning to do he could have died.

End of story. He got his exit visa eventually and left Egypt for good, and I cried for days. I went to Alexandria for the weekend to a lovely lady who I adored, stayed with her and her husband, and was fed champagne and told to sleep a lot, to forget!

Which, of course, I eventually did, but dreamt of M.S. for years, and I think it is the man I loved the most in all my life. Amen

He died in Paris a few years later, and I got a letter from him after he had died, I was working for Miss Arden in her Chicago Salon then, and it was a terrible shock for me, and very sad indeed.

Post Revolution. Impersonating "A day at ASCOT" charity affair.

Model wearing one of our creations.

CHAPTER 8

In 1957 my husband and I were able to take our summer vacation in Europe. We went to Italy with a friend of ours Lilliane, who lived in New York, but had grown up in Egypt.

Our first stop was in the beautiful Isle of Capri which we had never been to previously. As we arrived to the famous Piazza of Capri, Lilliane introduced us to a friend of hers Claude Fisher whom she knew from New York. The moment I laid eyes on him, I felt my legs trembling, and could not understand what was happening to me.

We then walked to our hotel "La Pinetta" and we were given a room in the annex, and Lillianne's room was in the main hotel. I immediately called Lilliane in her room to ask her to change rooms and join us in the annex. The phone in her room was picked up by Claude who was there with his wife. His voice washed through my body, it was deep and melodious. I felt my legs trembling again, and again I could not understand what was happening to me!

Later on we all had dinner together in one of those wonderful small restaurants facing the sea, and where the atmosphere was ever so romantic when the Italian "minstrels" proceeded to sing love songs accompanied by a guitarist . . . my legs trembled again! Next morning I tried to understand what I felt and surmised that I had a case of "love at first sight"! I was totally crazed!

That next day we all went to the "Canzone del Mare", a fabulous establishment on the other side of Capri, with a beautiful pool not too far from the Mediterranean.

Capri is such a fabulous island, it is breathtaking and beautiful . . . and ever so romantic.

My heart sank when I found out that Claude had gone to the mainland and that I would not see him that day. For my luck after that and for the 2 weeks we spent in Capri, we all were always together, at the Canzone or in the restaurants for lunch or dinner.

Ismail was in 7th heaven, because Capri and the "Canzone" specially was the location of all the best looking men in Europe, parading their tanned beautiful bodies.

As for myself, I did not know what was happening to me, I could not think of anything or anyone but Claude. One night as we were dancing in one of the famous nightclubs, he asked me if I knew what the meaning of the word "Yoga" was. I said I did practice yoga but had no idea what the meaning of the word itself was. He answered, it means "union" and added, "I would love to do yoga with you"! I was stunned and so happy to realize that he seemed to feel the same as I did.

From then on, and for the rest of our vacation, Claude and I took "Sandolinos" (small charming wooden row boats) every day and went for long hours rowing or swimming around all the Capri grottos. It was heaven. On August 15th of that year we ended up in one of the grottos, and Claude took me in his arms and kissed me.

I felt wonderful, it seemed like I had discovered a soul mate, and I started to fall totally in love with him.

Those were dreamy fantastic days of sun, sea, happiness, love and fun. Never to be forgotten by me. I was in love, and I believe he was also. Unfortunately all good things do have to end and the long winters back in Cairo seemed to me very dreary, but we corresponded constantly and kept our feelings mostly alive.

The next year when we applied for a visa to go to Europe on a buying trip for the shop only I was given the authorization to travel, as our shop was in my name.

Of course, I went to Capri, knowing the Fisher's would probably be there, but Claude had gone to Greece with friends, and I was terribly disappointed.

That same summer we met again in Paris and had wonderful times together, all too short to my liking, but always in romantic settings, like rowing in the bois de Boulogne, or touring the countryside. Every minute was filled with love and laughter and happiness, and felt like heaven on earth.

The miracle of LOVE

In Cairo, life began to be more difficult for us all, as Nasser ruled Egypt with an iron fist, and all the ex-upper class strongly felt its effect.

Of course we all tried to make the best of it and took our fate with dignity and resignation. Claude would come for a few days in winter to Egypt on business, and we enjoyed together a few moments of happiness and delight.

Meanwhile our shop turned out to be a great success, and gave me personally the only moments I looked forward to with great anticipation . . . times I spent with Claude in Italy, France, Switzerland in summer.

Years went by, my children were growing up, and in 1954 I had had a boy: Hassan, whom I had always yearned for, having until then only girls in our family.

I spent the next few years in Egypt except for the summers when I was in Paris and Italy buying stuff for our shop, to be copied in Egypt for our customers. At the back of my mind I still yearned to live in Europe, and made all the necessary efforts in order to achieve my goal. It certainly was not easy, as it was more and more difficult to obtain an exit visa unless one was over 60, or very ill, or had a business reason to travel. Of course I was determined to go abroad every summer, mainly to spend time with Claude.

At one point Nasser was having a reunion of all his ambassadors in India, and the good fashion houses of Egypt were asked to organize fashion shows in New Delhi and Bombay to promote Egyptian long staple cotton.

Of course we were asked to take part in the trip, so I was in charge of 18 beautiful Egyptian models, I would lock them into their rooms at night in the hotel so as to keep them from going out with all the Indian men who wanted to meet them and date them.

The second day of our arrival in Bombay I bumped into our ambassador to Iran, Mahmoud Hammad, and we had dinner together. He was a great friend of Ismail and myself, as he had been in Paris working at our embassy at the same time as Ismail had.

After dinner was over he asked me to have dinner the next night with a friend of his who happened to be a close friend of Nasser's. I accepted with pleasure, and the next night at 7 o'clock Hammad called me in my room at the Taj Mahal hotel and said he could not make the dinner as Nasser at the last minute had conveyed all of his ambassadors to dinner. So could I have dinner with H.H.? I accepted. H.H. and I therefore had dinner in the hotel's large dining room, and I dreaded it slightly as my Arabic was not up to par with H.H.'s and I told him so. "I'm of the old regime" I said, "and I don't speak Arabic well, so let's speak English".

Nevertheless we got along very well, so much so we ended up until 3 a.m. in the beautiful gardens of the hotel, H.H. reciting Arabic poetry to me which I understood not one word of.

As a matter of fact H.H. had been appointed by his boss to choose and buy a sari for his wife, His boss happened to also be a friend of mine and before I left Cairo had asked me, if I would meet H.H. in Bombay to help him buy the sari for his wife as he was sure I would do a better job than H.H.

So the next day H.H. and I proceeded to go shopping in Bombay for the famous sari, and by the time we found it we had become good friends.

This friendship continued and grew when we were all back in Cairo, and H.H. was a wonderful friend to me and helped me get a visa every time I needed one to go on my buying trips, for which I was really most grateful.

Meanwhile things were getting more difficult in Egypt, a lot of our friends were sequestrated, all their goods and properties were confiscated and some were even put in jail.

One felt the change in our society very strongly and there was quite a lot of anxiety in the air. As I had always wanted to live elsewhere, I remember thinking more and more about doing so, and one day as I awakened from my afternoon nap, and lay in bed dreaming, I saw in my two hands holding a sphere, the sphere was my life, and I thought, "my hands hold my life, and only I am going to be able to make my dream of leaving Egypt definitely come true. No one is going to help me but myself!"

From that day on, all my thoughts and efforts were pointed that way.

The year was 1965, and that summer I decided to take somewhat of a sabbatical and stay in Paris more than usual to supposedly find a job. I stayed in Paris for 6 months, living with the Martins who now had a beautiful apartment in Neuilly and, as usual, and actually since I first met them were ever so nice to me and hospitable. I was really lucky. After 6 months of knocking at every door to find a job to no avail I had almost decided to go back to Egypt disappointed when Tania Shahin (my best friend from Cairo) who had telephoned me from New York and asked me to go spend Christmas with her in New York as she had left Egypt the previous year and had been lucky enough to be introduced to Elizabeth Arden by some Russian friend, Evangeline Zaleski. Arden had hired her as fashion buyer for her salons, and Tania seemed to be doing a relatively good job.

That was Miss Arden, she liked foreign, elegant and sophisticated women to be around her and to work for her, whether they had any experience of the business or not. She believed her instincts and hired them on the spur of the moment.

I accepted Tania's invitation, and of course was dying to see Claude on his own turf. The second day I arrived Miss Arden invited me to dinner in her apartment on 5th Avenue and proceeded to immediately offer me a job. "Would you like to manage my San Francisco salon" she asked me. I was stunned, but firmly said no to her saying "for me New York is already the end of the world Miss Arden, so you can imagine what San Francisco would be". She said, "But you could go and come from San Francisco as you pleased". I said "No Miss Arden, I have to put my affairs in order with the Egyptian government first and then I can come back" It will only take me a month or two!"

Instead of staying 15 days in New York with Tania, I spent 3 months, and enjoyed every minute of it. I saw Claude often and he took me for a long weekend to Los Angeles where I had lunch with Queen Nazli (mother of King Farouk) and her youngest daughter

Fathia, whom we called "Atti" and had a really wonderful time. At the end of 3 months the time had really come for me to go back home, which I did reluctantly.

Little did I know what was in store for my there.

My 3 children, my husband and myself
just before leaving for New York. 1965.

Me and a group of models in India.

CHAPTER 9

I should go back now in time to a few previous years when I had made the decision to leave Egypt, but did not really know how to make that huge step.

As luck would have it, our best friends in Cairo were the Canadian ambassador and his wife, and they were transferred to Moscow. They were nice enough to tell me that if I wanted to take anything out of Egypt, they would be happy to do it for me as it could all go with their own belongings. In a strange way that prompted me to become very serious about my leaving my country for good, and I thanked them profusely. I started thinking about nothing else but leaving.

So I planned my departure very seriously, and in so doing had to find out how to do it. On week days I would go to the Canadian Embassy for lunch, and as they had a big pool in their gardens, I carried with me huge beach bags, supposedly filled with my bathing suits and towels . . . instead of which they were filled with silver, jewelry, etc, and anything I could think of that would be useful to me in Europe, or saleable.

Every time I passed in front of their gate my heart was really beating as of course they were guarded by "chaouichs" military personnel, and I dreaded being arrested by the chaouichs or being asked to open my beach bags. Thank God, no one blinked an eye and I was able to deliver all I wanted safely to the Canadian Embassy—Ouf! What a relief! On weekends the ambassadors would come to lunch in my mother's country estate near the Pyramids to swim in her pool. They also carried huge beach bags, which I, of course, proceeded to fill with all kinds of treasures which I felt I would need in my future life.

The difficulty occurred when I wanted to take all my oriental carpets, I had to really think hard to find a way of doing it. The opportunity arose when the ambassadors accepted an invitation to spend a weekend at my sister Doddy's country house near Alexandria.

The ambassador, his wife and myself left Cairo in their car driven by their chauffeur, and when we reached Alexandria, we made a bee line for the antique market. Of course we bought nothing, but upon returning to the car the ambassador's wife told her husband (who had stayed with the car waiting for his wife and I) that she had purchased some beautiful carpets that were going to be delivered that evening to Nevine's grandparent's home.

In fact, my sister and her husband brought all my carpets from Cairo in their car and we all met at 7 p.m. in my grandmother's garden. The ambassador, his wife and I had spent the afternoon in their car navigating the "corniche" of Alexandria several times to wait until

Doddy and her husband called us when they reached my granny's house in Alexandria. My sister told the ambassadors that a huge amount of boxes had been delivered from the market, and they in turn told their driver to put all the boxes in their car and go back to the embassy in Cairo, as they planned to spend the weekend in my sisters country house and would go back to Cairo in her car.

Ouf! What a relief again! Mission accomplished!

Finally, I could now really plan my departure, and felt a little better about the whole thing.

If you have never left your country for good, your family, your background, your life and your children to go to live as a woman alone in a foreign country you cannot imagine what a trauma it can be. The uncertainty and the sadness of it all is more than one would ever want to experience. But I was determined to do so since I was age 15, and I felt that nothing could stop me now.

Little could I foresee how it would all work out, but I was ready, willing and able to try.

It took me 9 bloody months to obtain an exit visa and I became totally obsessed with the idea of leaving my country, I could think of nothing else. During those 9 months I was interrogated several times by arrogant officers in dingy basements, about why I was going to Europe so often, what I was doing on a certain date in Switzerland, and who I was seeing from the foreign diplomatic corps. Of course this was very unnerving and very upsetting, and frightening. It made me feel scared, and almost a prisoner in my own country. Not a good feeling.

I finally decided to make one more effort and called H.H. to see if I could come and see him the next day in his office. That was going to be, in my mind, the last time I was going to ask for any favors from anyone.

I spent ½ hour in his office the next morning, pleading my case and the next thing I knew was that I burst into uncontrollable tears (which is unlike me), and left his office, and drove to the Pyramids and the desert to calm down.

At 2 o'clock when I came home for lunch my 10 year old son told me that I had been called by the passport office. I could not believe my ears. That afternoon I called H.H. to thank him and he said "Ah but there are strings attached, either you go and never come back, or you never go and stay in Egypt". I answered, "I hope you are joking because I'm not, but my answer would be "I stay here and never leave, I have 3 children and am not about to abandon them". He replied, "You can leave and with no strings attached". That was maybe one of the happiest days of my life, but also one of the saddest when I finally did depart. My mother, my children and Doddy and my husband accompanied me to the airport and I never stopped crying during the flight until I reached my first stop which was Paris.

Canadian Ambassador talking to me and H.H. in power.

CHAPTER 10
New York 1965

I stopped in Paris to rest a little before going to New York for good. Tanya called me and urged me to come to New York immediately, as she had come to know that there was a good job available for me at Ardens and if I was not there to take it, Miss Arden would most certainly hire someone else instead of me.

So I changed my ticket and landed in New York the next day. It had taken me 9 months to get the authorization to leave Egypt, but I had done it at last. I had dinner with Miss Arden soon after and she asked me if I would consider managing her fashion department in her salon on 5th Avenue. Of course, I said, I'd love to, and considered myself extremely lucky to find a job, one day after my arrival in this most fabulous city.

I told Miss Arden though that being Egyptian I had no working papers, no green card, etc. And she answered "Don't worry dear, if I have to go to the President himself, I will get these papers for you". So here I was, at last, in New York and with a job to boot.

I must say that I felt very lucky indeed. My first days in New York were wonderful, but I felt slightly sad as I saw very little of Claude and wondered what was happening to our relationship.

Evidently something was wrong, but I had some difficulty at understanding it. After all, Claude was one of the main reasons why I had tried so hard to leave Egypt. After a while Miss Arden sent me to Chicago as she had a new salon there, and she wanted me to learn my job, until I could really do it in New York.

I loved Chicago, I found the people charming and cultured and the pace less fast, furious and hectic than in New York. I met a lot of people who became great friends and really had a ball. I'll never forget the day that Miss Arden appeared in the salon, coming from San Francisco and spent the whole day in the Chicago salon examining everything, and criticizing a lot of it. I must admit that I was slightly in awe of her, and felt that I was expected to do my best so as not to lose my job. What a challenge, but then I have always loved challenges, and that was certainly a huge one.

Tania had warned me that if Miss Arden asked me for dinner, I should accept even if I had a date with the most charming man in Chicago. So that first day Miss Arden's niece, Pat Young" who always accompanied her aunt everywhere she went, told me "Dear, if Miss Arden asks you to dinner tonight, please refuse as she is very tired from her trip from San Francisco". Well, I hoped and prayed she would not ask me for dinner. Sure enough at 7 o'clock, she engulfed herself in her limo, and the door still open she asked me, "Dear, would you like to have dinner with me at the hotel tonight?" Wow, I really had a dilemma, whose advice shall I take, I wondered, Tania's or Pat Young's.

Truly I did not feel like having dinner with Miss Arden, so hesitantly, I said, "Miss Arden, I think I'll ask you for a rain check, as you are surely tired after the long journey from San Francisco". The car door was slammed shut, and that was the end of it.

The "Empress" was mad at me, and I expected to be fired the next day! Little did I know that I would work for her for the next 7 years, and also meet love again and my future husband!

The days went by quite agreeably, everyone was extremely nice to me, and I started to get quite happy with my job, and my new surroundings. I got invited to a lot of people's homes and truly formed quite a few solid friendships in that wonderful city. I spent a whole month there, and was told by Miss Marr, the Chicago salon manager, that she had been told to send me back to New York the next day. That same night I got invited by a famous architect I had met, to see a play with him and some friends of his, and enjoyed the evening tremendously. We stayed up until 3am and the next morning as I was boarding the plane back to New York, a hostess came to me, handed me a quarter and a telephone number to call . . . It was Miss Marr telling me that Miss Arden had just called to say I should stay longer in Chicago. So off the plane I went, and had lunch that day with the nice architect! Needless to say, we became very good friends and he was really most charming.

Eventually I returned to New York where I was living with Tania in a charming apartment at 130 E 65ᵗʰ Street, and finally started my new job. That first day was real scary, no one was there to introduce me to all the sales ladies, and I did not yet have the nerve to let them know I was their new manager. When Tania and I took a cab to go home at 5 o'clock, I told the taxi driver who asked us where he should drive us, "Bellvue would be just as good, if you would drive us there" I said. "I feel I've been at Bellvue all day already". But that was my first day. Things eventually became much easier as I was striving to do a good job, as usual, and meet the challenge.

3 months after I joined Arden's, we were introduced to our new manager for the salons, his name was Bill Miller. He was handsome, nice and American as apple pie. When Tania asked me, in an undertone, what I thought of him, I answered, "He is much too American for me!" Little did I know that I was to spend the next 45 years with him, loving every minute of it.

Our wonderful love affair was about to start.

Bill, of course, loved his vodka at cocktail time, as most Americans do, and Tania also loved her vodka as all Russians do. Tania also, I'm sure, felt that in order to secure her job she should befriend the boss. So she often asked Bill for a drink in our apartment after work, which he always accepted. Hating to be alone, and loving his vodka also.

So it became almost a routine, and he would appear at our doorstep very often at 6 o'clock—around 8 o'clock Tania would say, "I have to leave you both as I have a dinner engagement" and off she went. So I was left with Bill, who, not wanting to have dinner alone was almost forced to ask me to go out with him for dinner. As I had nothing better to do I would, of course, accept his invitations. That happened quite often, as Bill was alone in New York, his wife and family having stayed in Chicago until the end of the school year, for the children.

At the beginning I felt quite shy about the whole thing, but as time went on I started to look forward to those dinners and rather enjoyed them. Bill was quite entertaining, and his charm grew on me.

After a few months of this routine, I believe he enjoyed our dinners also, and we always had a lot to talk about, and started to really enjoy each other's company. In June of that year, he finally asked me to come to his hotel for dinner. I said I couldn't as I was supposed to have dinner that night with Tania, some friends of hers and of all people, the attorney general. What a boring dinner that was for me, especially as I was thinking of the nice time and dinner that I could have had with my boss.

After dinner the attorney general took us home in a cab, and Tania proceeded to ask him to come up for a night cap . . . which, of course, he did. I was furious, as they sat in the living room (which was my bedroom) and I retired immediately, sulking, to sleep in Tania's bedroom. I was in bed and almost asleep when I heard a knock on my door. It was Bill whom Tania had called and told him that I was sulking, and asked him to come over. Well, he came into my bedroom and one thing led to another and we both had a wonderful night of it. All's well that ends well! However, nothing was ending, it was just the beginning.

The next day, Bill and I had lunch at the "Italian Pavilion", our mood was great, we were dreamy eyed and felt wonderful. That is really the way it all started. 45 years of happiness which I will never ever forget.

Bill's love for me grew more and more as time went by, and after a few months we were both madly in love with each other. We would see each other every day at work, and somehow never had enough of each other. Problems started to arise though, there were too many obstacles to separate us; the company, his job, his wife and children, etc . . . Nothing was easy but our love was more important to both of us than anything else, it had become almost what mattered the most for both. We simply could not help it.

Tanya & Elizabeth Arden at a fashion show.

CHAPTER 11

This year was 1966 and Nimet, my oldest daughter came to live in New York. She stayed with Tania and me, at the beginning, but then was accepted at Columbia University where she proceeded to do in 2 years what the U.S. students would do in 4.

That summer Nihal and Hassan also came to New York to spend a month with me and loved it. We spent a week near Lake Paradox in the Adirondacks at a friend's house and really enjoyed it. Luccia, the owner, had inherited the house, and I had been going there very often to spend the weekends after work. It was a charming old house on the lake, so we swam, and canoed on Lake Paradox and had a lovely time. Luccia was a sales lady from Elizabeth Arden and we had become great friends because of our mutual love of music. Meanwhile my love affair with Bill grew and we became inseparable, and loved each other tremendously. It was simply marvelous and we enjoyed it immensely.

The days and years went by and we could not see enough of each other, but there was always the fear of being found out, and that would have probably ended our jobs at Elizabeth Arden. Anyhow, we spent a whole lot of time together, and grew fonder of each other all the time. Of course, having a "back street" affair is not the easiest of experiences. After 6 months, living with Tania was not the best solution, so I found an apartment on 73rd Street and 2nd Avenue to rent and loved it. At the same time Bill and his family lived quite nearby on 74th Street. So we'd often meet in the early a.m. and walk through Central Park to the office together. Those were always great moments spent together, that I will never forget. We loved each other deeply, and could not bear to be apart. The miracle of love!

One day Bill's wife, Patty, called me and asked to come and see me. Of course, I acquiesced but was extremely tense and nervous about the whole thing. I put on my best dress and waited for her arrival anxiously. She stepped out of the elevator and I wondered then what I would tell her. She started to tell me that "Bill was a great flirt, but this time it was not a flirtation", she felt he was deeply "in love", of course, I had to deny it all, and felt very guilty in so doing. His wife was a nice and pretty blond lady and I really did not like the role I had to play, and the lies I had to tell. But there was no other way, it was a real dilemma, I was not ready to let it all crumble. We ended the conversation after 1 hour and my advice to her was "Patty, you have to fight, that is the only solution". And I meant it.

My feelings for Bill were too strong and I could not bear the idea of stopping it all. Neither could he. I tried to tell him that we should stop seeing each other, he said yes we should, and the day after at 5 o'clock he called me on the 2nd floor at Arden's saying, "And how about a drink at the Mayfair in half an hour. And so it was! And we loved it. We were immensely happy. After a few years of that "regime" none of us could really take it anymore. Thank God Patty met a wonderful man who was an ex admiral of the Navy. They fell in love and decided to get married.

Bill came to my apartment that afternoon and said to me in a triumphant voice, "I have had the biggest raise I've had in my life, Patty is getting married". Hurrah I screamed! We were both so happy, it was wonderful. A month later we also decided to get married. Of course I had to quit my job at Arden's, as my job was not as important as his, and 2 persons of the same family were not allowed to work in the same segment of the company.

So here it was finally. My life had come full circle, I was getting married again, and to an American. My Muslem divorce from Ismail was not recognized in New York state, so we decided to get married in our friends home, the Restin's, who lived in Fairfield, CT.

CHAPTER 12

The wedding itself was a very simple affair, unlike my first wedding in Cairo. There was a luncheon at the Restin's house in Fairfield, only attended by our 2 families. 3 of Bill's children, Nimet, my daughter and my niece and husband and my nephew. We all drove later to New York harbor as Bill and I were going to the Caribbean on a cruise ship for our honeymoon. I remember that it was pouring rain that day, but everyone told us that it was a very good omen for our marriage. We had about 40 guests who came to the boat to drink champagne with us and wish us all the happiness in the world.

My best friend Joanne had to come by bus as there were no cabs available because of the rain, and being a native New Yorker she managed to convince the bus driver to drive the bus away from its usual circuit and let her out in front of our boat. They were both from Irish descent, so that was a help. It was all great fun and both Bill and I were so happy. Finally, the great event had happened and we were really married, and hoping to live a wonderful life together. And we indeed had a fabulous marriage, we were very much in love with each other, and really blessed to be together.

The Egyptian and the American, each with such a different background. It was really the miracle of love. And we truly loved each other dearly. Of course, we had been living together in New York when we came back from our honeymoon after 2 weeks, we were already totally used to our new lives and to each other. These were great days indeed, of happiness and love.

I had had to quit my job at Elizabeth Arden but had immediately been hired by Montaldo's as a lingerie buyer for their 20 stores, and life went on in a very pleasant way. 1 year later someone called me from the market to ask me if I was happy with my job, and if not, did I want to have an interview with Bergdoff Goodman for the same job. I said yes, of course! When I said that to Bill that night, he looked at me strangely and said, "You are a foreigner, you don't really know what you're doing, and they will promote from within"! I answered, "I don't care, and I'm going to that interview". So I went, slightly scared and had the interview. It all went so well they then asked me when I could work for them, and I readily answered "in 2 weeks probably, so I have time to finish my buy with Montaldo's". I came home that night, we were living in a lovely apartment on 72nd Street with a terrace and as we were sipping our cocktails, I told Bill I thought I would be hired by Bergdoff. He answered, "Well, I've just come from talking to the president of Elizabeth Arden and he is sending me to London as head of Elizabeth Arden international". I could not believe my ears, but I said to Bill "I'm still going to go tomorrow morning to meet the President of Bergdoff and see if I have the job just to prove you wrong! And I did! And got the job! And had to go back the next day to tell them I could not take it as I was going to London with my husband because of his new job!

We spent 5 years in London, and they were a dream. We lived in a most beautiful penthouse duplex apartment overlooking Hyde Park, between the Dorchester Hotel and the Hilton. The height of luxury and comfort. They were probably the happiest years of our lives. Totally different from New York, but wonderful. So much culture, theatre, concerts and a grand piano in the living room on which I practiced on every day. Fabulous! The English are so civilized, and we absolutely had a great life in London and met so many lovely people who became great friends. And, of course, we entertained constantly and I loved it! And I think I did it also very well, so everyone said at least. Bill had stopped smoking, instead he smoked cheap American cigars "Anthony & Cleopatra"! And every guest who came to stay with us was forced to bring us a box of Anthony & Cleopatra. Our freezer had nothing else in it but cigar boxes.

The apartment was superb, a duplex with 4 bedrooms, 4 ½ bathrooms, living room, dining room, office, and den. Most fabulous. And views of the park to boot!

We stayed in London from 1976 to 1981, and unfortunately in 1978 I had the worst experience of my life. Hassan's accident.

One morning, Bill was already at work, and my cousins, the Shahin's, were spending a few days with us. They stormed into my bedroom at 9am and told me that my son, Hassan in Cairo, had suffered a terrible accident, totaled the car he was driving, and totaled himself as well. He was in a coma in the general hospital but still alive. Thank God.

Nothing is as awful as anything happening to one's children, the anxiety and sadness one goes through is such, that it is almost unbearable of course, I rushed to Cairo, and was shocked to see my only son, the "apple of my eyes" in such a terrible state. Arms, legs and hips broken. Not speaking at all and so near death. He stayed in that hospital for 1 month after which, was allowed to come to London accompanied by his sister, Nihal, and by a friend of his, Dr. Samir Fanous. I felt better when he arrived in London as we found through friends a wonderful hospital "St John & St. Elizabeth" and an excellent orthopedic surgeon, Mr. Michael Lawrence. He spent 4 months in that hospital, and I went every day to spend hours and hours with him, to cheer him up.

Finally he came out of it, all thanks to the wonderful care he was given by everyone involved. Those were really painful days of worry, uncertainty and sadness. But all went well and he was starting to make real progress. After 4 months he was able to come home to us and was so happy to be alive and better. What a dreadful experience it had all been. And how lucky we all were to have been able to have him looked after by wonderful doctors and nurses. We got a special nurse to stay with him at home and soon the nightmare started to dissipate. What a blessing that was.

Meanwhile Bill and I decided to charter a boat on the Thames for a week, and take a well-deserved mini holiday. We spent the night on board, and at 8 o'clock the next morning started to try and go through the first lock. Bill was at the helm and I picked up the bow line and jumped ashore to attach the boat to the shore. I was wearing boots (not boat shoes unfortunately) and fell upon reaching the ground. I pulled up my jeans, and there in front of me were my 2 bones staring at me. What a shock that was. An ambulance was called and came to

Redding, where we were, and drove us to the nearest hospital. There I was operated upon and ended up with my whole leg in a cast!

Not a very pleasant occurrence with a patient at home already. I had to learn to use crutches and was told it would only take 6 weeks to heal . . . Well it took 6 months! What a bore! But thank God I was very well looked after and was able to resume my life after 6 months.

London had not lost its appeal for us and we still enjoyed every bit of it. I only have fabulous memories of those days, and we both cried the day Bill was transferred back to New York at the head office.

American wedding to Bill Miller.

CHAPTER 13

Our life in New York was very pleasant though, and we soon began to like it again and enjoy it. We rented a 1 bedroom apartment on 52nd Street near the East River, and had our country house in Weston Connecticut where we enjoyed our weekends.

It was an old most charming house from 1776, low ceilings, small windows, tight stairs, which we had bought at the start of our marriage, and that we had totally remodeled by a wonderful architect while we were in London. He did a wonderful job, we had a 2 acre garden with a pond, lots of frogs, and a swimming pool was added after living there for a few months. We would go there every weekend, and had lots of friends visit us often. All in all great fun and great years.

I then decided I had had enough of the fashion world and took a course in real estate and got hired at once by a real estate firm by the name of Sulzberger-Rolfe. Soon I became very successful in my job, and specialized in the sale of condominiums, as I dealt mostly with foreigners, and condos were easier than co-ops for them to buy. I really loved my job, and was far more interested in real estate than in being a fashion buyer.

I had lots of clients because of all the people we knew, friends, Elizabeth Arden clients, and lots of foreigners like myself.

Of course by then I had become a U.S. citizen and all was very OK with the world. Wonderful life, wonderful husband, wonderful children, wonderful friends and lots of happiness and loads of fun. I was blessed from my childhood until now, and very lucky indeed to have succeeded in such a great country as the U.S.

Bill was proud of me, and I loved him dearly.

The years went by swiftly and everything seemed to be quite easy for us.

Bill took his retirement in 1986, and I continued in real estate but changed from Sulzberger-Rolfe to MJ Raynes and loved my new company and all the friends I made. I had succeeded in my new life, I was a happy camper in the "New World". How lucky can you get?

We had bought a small condo in Florida on a beautiful island called Boca Grande in 1979, and started to go there often from New York for a few days or weeks of R & R.

As a matter of fact, my cousin, Ismail who attended my 2nd wedding said of me, "you are like a lion tamer, you like men with strong characters, opinionated and tough acting and you enjoy breaking/taming them until they finally eat out of your hand. Makes life interesting and certainly challenging!"

CHAPTER 14

Boca Grande

Boca Grande Island is 7 miles long and 3 ½ miles wide, it is a beautiful island on the Gulf of Mexico on the Southwest coast of Florida. We had been told about it by the Hanley's who were great friends, and Will Hanley had also been the president of Elizabeth Arden. They had visited us a few times while we were in London, and we had become all very fond of each other. My first impression of Boca Grande was not the greatest, but Bill loved it the moment he arrived, and was very keen on buying a condo in the new Club that was being built.

I for one was not, at first, as enthusiastic and told Bill, "Its only palm trees and sand, too much like Egypt"! After spending 3 days there though my first impression changed. And upon getting back to London, I immediately called my sister Doddy in Paris to ask her to tell her husband I needed money. Mahmoud, my brother-in-law, had always looked after my affairs, since my father had died, and he was a most charming and delightful man. It turned out that he had finally been able to sell the land my father had so generously given his children, and the money was there waiting for me. So, 1 week after, Bill and I went back to Boca Grande and bought Marina Village #8. It was a most charming condominium on Charlotte Harbor, and we grew to love Boca Grande tremendously. We met lovely people who all became great friends, we had a boat, and Bill went fishing often and was as happy as a clam. And we have been living there ever since. And loving it!

The climate is perfect, the people are delightful, hospitable, nice and fun to be with.

This is the end of my story. I've had the most fabulous life, I've made it exactly what I planned to make it, and I've been one happy person living it up through thick and thin, and creating for myself and family quite a few wonderful and great memories! Since 1966 until the present, my life in my new country has been the greatest. Lots of love, happiness, fun. Wonderful friends, great husband, lovely children, fantastic step children and best of all, living in the United States for almost 60 years, I cannot help appreciating this country for all it has given me, and the super life I have led.

Nevine and Bill in Boca Grande, Florida.

GOD BLESS AMERICA THE END 2/23/2013—Boca Grande

The author.